**The Unfinished
Harauld Hughes**

WORKS BY HARAULD HUGHES

plays

PLATFORM

TABLE

ROAST

ROOST

PROMPT

FLIGHT

SHUNT

DEPENDENCE

prose/pieces

SPEECH

THE SITTING-DOWN DOOR (A PLAY WITHOUT WORDS)

screenplays

THE SWINGING MODELS

THE ESPECIALLY WAYWARD GIRL

THE MODEL AND THE ROCKER

THE TERRIBLE WITCH

THE AWFUL WOMAN FROM SPACE

THE DEADLY GUST

THE GLOWING WRONG

O BEDLAM! O BEDLAM! (unfinished)

poetry

THE WOUND, THE WOODS, THE WELL:

THE COLLECTED POEMS OF HARAULD HUGHES 1957–1977

The Unfinished
Harauld Hughes

RICHARD AYOADE

faber

First published in 2024
by Faber & Faber Ltd
The Bindery, 51 Hatton Garden
London ECIN 8HN
First published in the USA in 2024

Typeset by Ian Bahrami
Printed in the UK by CPI Group (UK) Ltd, Croydon CRO 4YY

Extracts from *Herstory: My Time with Harauld Hughes* (2010) by
Lady Virginia Lovilocke, reproduced by permission of Loveco Ltd, London
Extracts from the letters and notebooks of Leslie Francis are reproduced
courtesy of the Estate of Leslie Francis

The right of Richard Ayoade to be identified as author
of this work has been asserted in accordance with Section 77
of the Copyright, Designs and Patents Act 1988

A CIP record for this book
is available from the British Library

ISBN 978-0-571-37789-3

Printed and bound in the UK on FSC® certified paper in line with our continuing
commitment to ethical business practices, sustainability and the environment.
For further information see faber.co.uk/environmental-policy

2 4 6 8 10 9 7 5 3 1

CONTENTS

DRAMATIS PERSONAE

OUR HERO
Harauld Hughes – playwright, poet, screenwriter

HIS LOVES
Felicity Stoat – actress, Hughes's first wife
Lady Virginia Lovilocke – theologian, chef, Hughes's second
  wife

HIS FAMILY
Ophelia Hughes – oft-lapsed nun, Hughes's mother
Mickie Perch – producer, nightclub owner, Svengali, Hughes's
  half-brother, twin brother of . . .
Colin Perch – accountant, business manager of Anglers
  Productions
Clifton 'Monkey' Perch – father of Mickie and Colin,
  stepfather to Hughes

HIS COLLEAGUES
Mick Barrett – actor, childhood friend of Hughes
Leslie Francis – documentarian, film theorist, director of
  Hughes's stage work and the films *And . . .?!* and *O Bedlam!*
  O Bedlam!
Ibssen Anderssen – pop photographer, director of *The Models*
  Trilogy, *The Awful Woman from Space*, *The Terrible Witch*,
  The Deadly Gust, *The Glowing Wrong*

Candy Doors – actress, Mickie Perch's third wife
Miloš Mareck – Leslie Francis's cinematographer
Donny Chapel – musician, composer

HIS CRITIC
Augustus Pink – theatre critic, Hughes's biographer

CURTAIN

Harauld Hughes's funeral was as terse as one of his plays. The boy who had come of age in the post-war rubble of Elephant and Castle was laid to rest in the arboreal hush of Brompton Cemetery.

At his request, the coffin was painted black.

The distinctly unceremonious ceremony was attended by only four people, two of whom were passers-by. There was no eulogy.

Attendees received a private printing of Hughes's *Complete Plays* and a miniature bottle of Slow Fade, his signature single malt. His second wife, Lady Virginia Lovilocke, though a Catholic and a lay theologian, did not read from the Bible, nor were there any religious readings. Instead, Hughes's only remaining friend, the actor Mick Barrett, read the final verse of Hughes's poem 'The Wound':

> There is no air.
> There is no ground.
> There is just the wound.
> It will not close.
> I won't allow it.

I

In their last conversation, already aware he had but weeks to live, Hughes had suggested Barrett read from another of his poems, 'Erosion', with its explosive opening . . .

> It turned to silt
> And washed away.
> It turned to shit
> And stuck.

But Hughes relented. Age, he said, had softened him. When Harauld Hughes died in 2006, he hadn't written a play for thirty-four years.

——————————

In Lady Virginia Lovilocke's memoir of her life with Hughes, *Herstory: My Time with Harauld Hughes*, she movingly attests to the mystery of the other:

> Like all biographies, this is a work of fiction. By which I mean, since we are all, in some ways, characters of our own creation, it is hardly surprising that our lives are replete with both invention and omission. More than anyone, Harauld insisted that we be truthful, but never have I met a man more committed to the serious business of play.

The reader, guided by Lady Lovilocke's deft hand, is acutely aware of the resonances of the word 'play' in such close proximity to Hughes's name, for Hughes was a poet known chiefly for his dramas; a political polemicist who loved badminton and did so much to restore the game to social prominence; and a gifted actor who became one of the most celebrated screenwriters of his generation. He wrote his first play, *Platform*, in 1960, but it was his fourth play, *Roost*, written, unusually, before his third play, *Roast*, that made his reputation. He remains one of the UK's most garlanded playwrights. He was awarded the Euripides Prize for short-form drama and the Goethe Garter, and was one of the first writers-in-residence at Costa Coffee, albeit in an unofficial capacity. He was also the celebrated screenwriter of such films as *The Especially Wayward Girl*, *The Deadly Gust* and *The Glowing Wrong*. There is drama before Harauld Hughes and there is drama after Harauld Hughes. For Harauld Hughes, to my mind, *is* drama.

————————

Harauld Hughes was born in Cardiff in 1931. The house in which he lived has since been demolished to accommodate a new trampoline park called Flip Zone ('For kidz aged 9–99!!'). With his broiling temperament and tendency for explosive outbursts, Hughes was his own kind of 'Flip Zone'; his mother, Ophelia, a missionary, also possessed an apocalyptic temper. Hughes finally spoke about his origins in this 1981 interview with the *Swansea Examiner*:

> My mother had evangelised with particular fury in Nigeria, localising much of her ire in the university town of Ibadan, where they now teach my work. After these purges of native devilry, she clearly felt compelled to slake her own spirits.
> She was maligned as a strumpet who cavorted with heathens in the bush, whereas I know for a fact that the identity of my father can be narrowed down to a group of no more than twenty or so, many of whom were highly regarded and had their own lodgings.

Upon discovering her pregnancy, Ophelia returned to England. The identity of Harauld Hughes's father was never resolved.

Because of the stigma, my mother was sent to Coventry, literally – she had family there. I can't imagine what she went through. It seems that no one in the Midlands is there voluntarily.

Incredibly for a nun, this was not Ophelia's first pregnancy. Before joining the sisterhood, she had secretly given birth to twins. She entrusted them to the sole care of their father, with whom she remained on friendly terms.

I was smuggled away to London by a 'friend' of my mother called Clifton Perch, a retired Nigerian sailor who was already in sole charge of twin boys, Mickie and Colin, also of mixed heritage.

Brooding, taciturn and possessed of incredible strength, Clifton 'Monkey' Perch was a merchant seaman on the Cardiff to Lagos cargo route. As well as undisguised racism, his nickname reflected his preternatural capacity for climbing the rigging. In 1917, the man who would become Harauld Hughes's de facto father survived a German U-boat attack by clambering up to the crow's nest and jumping onto a passing biplane, which he subsequently commandeered and used to destroy the submarine that had just sunk his ship. For this, he received two days' extra rations and the option to do more work above deck. He deserted and settled in Cardiff, becoming a signwriter for especially high-up billboards, often without using a platform. When he eventually fell, he was placed in a psychiatric hospital for suggesting that he needed medical attention.

While at Cardiff City Asylum, he met Ophelia Hughes, a trainee nurse, and as soon as he came out of traction, the two began an affair so torrid that it put him back in traction. Guilt-ridden, Ophelia left the nursing profession and decided to take holy orders. Perch, broken-hearted and broken-backed, would never climb again, resolving to raise his boys in ground-floor accommodation only. He needed lateral living space, and fast, so Perch became the live-in cook for a bohemian family whose terraced house in Elephant and Castle was slightly wider than average, due to a building defect that meant the property was slowly spreading.

He had been there barely a year when a basket arrived for him. A basket containing a boy. This latter-day Moses had a note round his neck: 'Room for one more? His name is Harauld Hughes. Keep him in God's Loving Mercy. Best regards, Ophelia.' 'Monkey' Perch took the boy in, setting up another crib in the dumb waiter.

Up until the outbreak of the Second World War, Hughes lived in the Elephant with Monkey, Mickie and Colin in a street called Brook Drive, now most famous for being the backdrop for the music video for Dexys Midnight Runners' relentless song 'Come On Eileen'. At one end of the road, a young Hughes could see the Lambeth workhouse that once housed Charlie Chaplin, while at the other lay the famous Bedlam asylum, closed only recently in 1930, and which lay abandoned until it became the home of the Imperial War Museum in 1936. In 1932, the Coronet cinema, a 2,000-seat art deco wonder, was built on the nearby Old Kent Road, opposite the even more impressive 3,000-seat Trocadero picture house, with its sumptuous George Coles interiors in the French Renaissance style. Hughes was to spend much of his youth sneaking in and out of these two cinemas, inhaling westerns, gangster films and musicals. Forty years later, Hughes would write a film called *O Bedlam! O Bedlam!*, which remains unfinished and represents not only his last work for the screen, but also his last in any medium. One could say that Hughes's life began and ended in the shadow of Bedlam. Perhaps that's what Hughes was thinking about when he once said, 'Our end must find its start in our beginning.'

1

LEAVING THE PLATFORM

                    ACTRESS
        I think you might be the most conceited
        man I've ever met.

                    ROCKER
        So you do agree we've met? We have
        become acquainted?

                    ACTRESS
        We're on the same platform.

From *Platform* (1960) by Harauld Hughes,
published by Faber & Faber

In Harauld Hughes's full-length debut, an actress stands breathless on the platform of what the stage directions identify as an 'isolated railway station somewhere in the north of England'. Sodden and tired, she is reluctant to talk to the only other person around, a cocksure musician (gnomically named 'Rocker' in the cast list), but unable to resist his provocations, she finds herself drawn into a disquisition on love, power and the illusions that keep us apart. More than sixty years after that play opened in London, I am trapped in an illusion of my own, pretending to be on a Journey of Discovery for a documentary called *The Unfinished Harauld Hughes*, because mindlessly going from one place to another allows us to ignore the fact that we lack a coherent narrative.

'It was Here,' I find myself shouting from our counterfeit railway platform, 'that Hughes had the idea that would change his life for ever. It was Here, in the winter of 1953, that he saw a woman running onto the platform, bedraggled from the rain, holding a large red suitcase.' Later, we'll film a reconstruction of this, in slow motion, for those unable to imagine what a woman might look like while running through the rain with a red suitcase. 'The woman was an actress, hoping to catch the last train to London, but she was too late. Hughes, watching the scene unfold, was so struck by the sight of what he would later call her "beguiling desperation" that he jumped out of the moving carriage. He had seen his future. A future called Felicity. Felicity Stoat. Within a year they will be married. And Stoat will go on to play the part of "Actress" in *Platform*, the play that will make Harauld Hughes's name.'

A pre-selected station guard blows a whistle, and the train pulls away long enough for the cameraman to get a shot of it pulling away, before the train stops and the rest of the crew get on board to film the fake Felicity Stoat pantomiming her late arrival. I turn to camera and, aided by an understated zoom, give it the full treatment . . .

'But, less than twenty-five years later, in the spring of 1977, Hughes was on a different platform with a different woman. A lady: Lady Virginia Lovilocke. This time, Hughes didn't disembark. And the platform wasn't a train platform. It was a helicopter landing pad. A helicopter landing pad hastily erected on the set of *O Bedlam! O Bedlam!*, a film Hughes had ripped from the book of his heart, a film that fell, famously, apart. One journey was an arrival that took Hughes towards his first marriage and an explosion of creativity without rival in the Post-War British Theatre. The other was a departure via divorce, the collapse of his career and a doomed attempt to reconcile two distinct worlds: the stage and the screen. Hughes found himself at a terminus from which he would never return.

8

He would not write again until his death thirty years later. So, what went wrong? Why does no one speak of Britain's most innovative dramatist? What in hell happened . . . to Harauld Hughes?'

I provide a visual counterpoint to my Mission Statement Voice-Over by gazing meaningfully out of the window, while dappled light plays on my pensive face.

'I want to get to know Harauld Hughes. Who he was, why he wrote and why he stopped.'

———————

I cannot remember when someone first mentioned the name Harauld Hughes to me, but I do remember when I was first told I looked like him.

I was panning for classics in a second-hand bookshop when I looked up to see the stress-pinked eyes of the bookshop owner, Keith, a piece of white chocolate softening in his ghostly hands.

'You have a double,' he said.

This used to happen often. People would say I reminded them of someone they knew. What they tended to mean was that they had once met another person whom they couldn't confidently categorise in terms of ethnicity – a variation on 'Where are you from, *originally*?'

I said either 'Oh' or 'Huh?' or 'Right', one of those barely communicative cul-de-sacs designed to bring conversation to a close, but Keith persisted.

'Look under "H",' he said. '"H" for Hughes.'

I held up a copy of *Birthday Letters*.

'Not that windswept bastard. Harauld. H. A. R. A. U. L. D. The mother was Welsh.'

I found the name on a spine. Harauld Hughes: *The Two-Hander Trilogy.*

'Look on the back,' Keith said.

I looked. I saw the author's picture.

I had a double. Even in profile, the resemblance was remarkable. It was me.

Of course, there was a variation in age. I was sixteen and, by that stage, had written only one or two major theatrical works. Hughes, pictured in a stark black-and-white photograph, looked to be in his thirties, had the command of a literary giant and wore the kind of glasses I would search for, in vain, from that moment on.

I opened the book and, on the inside of the dust jacket, saw the titles of the three individual plays:

Platform. Table. Shunt.

Aggressive, terse, mysterious. Within moments I was drawn into Hughes's sinister dance of suspicion and destruction.

'Would you like to read *all* of the book before you buy it?' said Keith, as he licked his upturned fingers; they were crooked, flesh stalagmites, waxed white.

But I had already finished the book and started another. A book of screenplays. How could someone write for the theatre *and* for the screen? It seemed impossible, yet Hughes had managed it. I saw each film unspool in my mind's eye. I was an instant acolyte. Hughes was my boy.

Now I have the responsibility, the honour, of introducing him to the next generation of visionaries. But how can I hope to show the 'truth' about anyone, let alone someone so shrouded in admiration and approbation? How can I prevent a descent into rote hagiography? How do I swerve the potholes of pretension, generality's broad brush or obscurantism's beckoning nook?

Why did I agree to participate in this documentary? Normally the answer would be 'money', but I haven't been paid yet. There isn't even a contract.

It seems that I'm doing this for the sheer love of Hughes.

———————

A few moments after we wrap, with the crew already packing away their gear, it strikes me that the sentence 'He would not write again until his death thirty years later' makes it sound like Hughes resumed writing in phantom form, his fleshless hand inking a quill, but I let it pass. We are in the van now, receded in separate cells of inwardness, trundling to the Travel Tavern.

2

TAKING THE MICK

```
                    MICK
You're binary. That's your downfall.
It's got to be either this or that.

                   CHARLIE
Well, what else can it be?

                    MICK
Neither this nor that.

                   CHARLIE
If it's not this and it's not that,
what is it?
```

From *Roast* (1964) by Harauld Hughes,
published by Faber & Faber

We are in Elephant and Castle, looking for a 'greasy spoon'-style cafe to replicate the kind of eatery frequented by Hughes and his 'Lambeth boys'. I'm about to meet Hughes's oldest friend. Nicknamed Mickie Two to avoid confusion with Mickie Perch, Mick Barrett was a core member of this five-strong group of lads comprising Hughes, the Perch twins and 'Tiny' Clive. The cafe we find has such a thick film of grease on every surface that I ask to sit on a tray. I order the 'Cooked 3', which is both varied and singular.

Barrett was the original 'Rocker' in the stage version of *Platform*, though he would be replaced by Donny Chapel in the television version (broadcast as part of a series called *The Harauld Hughes Half-Hour Play*). He played 'He' in *Table*, though in the television version he was (again) replaced, this time by Herbert

Sand, while Patrick Rusk reinterpreted 'Charlie' and 'Terry' in *Roast* and *Roost*, even though Barrett played them first. Barrett also missed out on reprising the role of 'Him' in the television iteration of *Flight* after Hughes took the proto-feminist decision to cast Felicity Stoat in the part (though the fact that he had given the role of 'She' to the increasingly high-profile 'starlet' Inger Marie, with whom he was having an affair, may have been the deciding factor). Despite these disappointments, Barrett remained loyal to Hughes until the end.

Dan, the director of our documentary (who refers to himself variously as 'D Man', 'D'Man' and 'D Dog'), is adjusting the frame with his aggressively reticent cameraman Tony, aka Tony Camera. The sound recordist, Wiggsy Sound, scratches the skin under his Slinky of leather bracelets, brings his fingers up to his nose and catches the bulk of the resultant cough in the palm of his hand. What's left, he wipes on his 'Sawdust Is Man Glitter' T-shirt before attaching my microphone pack. He apologises for his breath, before leaning in conspiratorially: 'I heard Mickie Two was quite the lad in his day. They called the Woolworth Road sexual health clinic the Mick Barrett Centre. People think Mickie Perch was King of the Bush, but Mickie Two got more tail than a taxidermist.' I thank Wiggsy for telling me such a beautiful story.

Stepping out of the Uber, Mick Barrett is less the strutting peacock of 1960s lore and more the chalk outline of a baby crow. His skin is dusty white, like a tired Pierrot. His obviously dyed hair, scraped into Brylcreemed heaps, looks like scorched scrub.

Attempting to accelerate intimacy, I extend a paw. Mick is not far south of ninety, but he seems older.

– How are you, Mick?
– Well, I'm still going. Just about.

– Thanks for agreeing to come.
– Well, I said I would, so I did.

Aptly, Barrett's last television performance was as 'Man Near Cafe' in *Medic, A.M.*, a procedural series set in the world of hospital radio that enjoyed a brief run in the late 1970s. Since then, he has been a freelance drama coach, the face (or should that be the 'back'?) of an osteoporosis infomercial and an assistant chiropodist ('I've always believed in feet').

Tony Camera is rolling; Wiggsy Sound's at speed; the cafe owner is primed to place two plates of breakfast in front of us as soon as Dan screams 'Action!' As is the way with television interviews, Mick has been instructed to incorporate my questions into his answers.

– You knew Harauld Hughes from a very young age. When did you first meet?
– I knew Harauld from a very young age.
– And when did you and Harauld first meet? You were quite young?
– When I first met Harauld, we were quite young.
– Do feel free to answer in your own way.
– I feel free to answer in my own way.

We cut. Mick tells us how he prefers raspberries to strawberries. This is not in response to the question 'Do you prefer raspberries to strawberries?' – he just thought we should know. It becomes clear that when it comes to information, Mick considers it better to give than to receive. We try again.

– Harauld saw things. He was different. He had those eyes.

They pierced you. Like a skewer, only they were eyes. We met up the Elephant. Mickie and Colin too. Only had two pairs of shorts between them. Then it was the war. He went east. I went west.

By 'west' he means Weymouth.

– Harauld offered to enlist. But they wouldn't take him because of his eyes.

They wouldn't take him because he was eight. Hughes was, in fact, evacuated to Ipswich.

– Where did Mickie and Colin go during the war?
– They stayed with Monkey in the Elephant. No one wanted twins. It was two too much by half. Mickie was a handful – he had form with the fuzz. Racketeering. Conspiracy to defraud. Assault with a deadly cosh.

Mickie was nine.

– And Monkey could barely move. He wouldn't go into the underground shelters neither. He hated depths almost as much as he hated heights. One night Monkey told the boys to leave him be. He had a flan that wanted doing, and they should clear right out if they knew what was good for them. When they came back, Monkey and the flan had been flattened by a bomb.
– That must have hit Hughes hard.
– Harauld was miles away. He was in Ipswich.
– I meant Monkey's death.

– Oh, Monkey didn't die. He just got flattened. It'd take more than a bomb to kill Monkey. He was a sinewy old shit. The flames took his eyelids, of course. Made it hard for him to get much kip.

– I didn't know.

– Oh yeah. He was very snappy.

– I didn't know he had no eyelids.

– I just told you he didn't have no eyelids.

– I suppose that's why he looks so intense in the photos I've seen.

– I don't know what photos you've seen.

– Did you hear from Hughes during the war?

– No. There was a war on, you see. Harauld started hanging around the RAF base at Martlesham. That's where he learned how to smoke and shout. His natural speaking voice got to be the equal of a fighter plane, which was good training for working in the round. In the end they made him a junior officer.

– What did he do?

– Fetching. Brewing up. Keeping 'em peeled. That's when he started to learn what a man was.

– Thirsty?

– I'm all right, thanks. When the war ended, they gave Harauld a full military discharge. Back he went. London town. We hadn't seen each other since we were nippers. Suddenly we were men.

They were fourteen.

– Monkey bought himself a cafe. It just did liver and kidneys and tripe. It was called the Offal Truth. Monkey had to cook up in the dark, with his shades on. Everything was too

17

bright for him, so a lot got spilt. He was knee-deep in guts.

– Was Harauld close to Mickie and Colin?

– Mickie was a force. He was out front, charming the birds. Giving it all this, that and the other. Colin was quieter. He did the accounts, which, as far as I could see, was just shoving all the receipts onto a spike and telling the taxman to do one. Harauld merely scrubbed and watched. He took it all in. He said scraping entrails off the floor prepared him for a life in show business. And there was Clive, who was tiny.

– What did he do?

– Nothing much. But his mum was a librarian, so he got us into books. Me and Harauld read everything. Could be Proust, could be a menu – we just loved language. And we pranced about. We were performers. People forget that about Harauld. He was an actor.

It puts me in mind of a Hughes quote:

Writing is acting. You pretend to be a writer. Just like you pretend to be a person.

(From *Actor/Writers on Writing and Acting: The Interviews, Vol. VI*, edited by Chloë Clifton-Wright, published by Faber & Faber)

– Did Mickie and Colin also read voluminously?

– Mickie didn't believe in reading. He considered it unmanly. And Col was into maths – he didn't see the point in words. I don't remember him ever saying anything.

– Nothing?

– Put it this way: I can't picture his mouth moving unless there was bacon in it.

– Was Harauld writing by that stage?

— Harauld was writing before he could talk. I can still remember the first poem he wrote.

Dan's eyebrows are raised in pre-emptive assent.

— Would you do us the honour of reciting it?
— I can't remember it. I just remember that he wrote it. It was called 'Ruck'. It was about fights. But, you know – for fun. No blades.

Hughes never wrote a poem called 'Ruck', though it sounds like something he could have written. I think the poem Barrett is referring to is this one:

> 'Bundle'
>
> The boy turned
> And saw them
> In the air,
> Faces stretched with
> An expanse of joy.
> No reason
> (Or perhaps
> He forgot his offence).
> Never mind, he was
> Underneath them now,
> With wind knocked out
> And tears down his nose.
> How long has it been
> Since they cleaned this
> Carpet?
>
> (From *The Wound, the Woods, the Well: The Collected Poems of Harauld Hughes 1957–1977*)

– We were always bundling. That's what did my back in – how I got the osteoporosis, the vertebrae all compacted. I got off lightly. Put it this way: 'Tiny' Clive started off tall. Still, it's better than being stretched – some of the lads round Stepney did that. It was just a way to pass the time. These days, they've got the internet. Even now I feel the urge to jump on someone from a height – you know, to loosen things up. The only rule was: you don't bundle Monkey. He's suffered enough.

– Did Harauld participate in these bundles?

– People see him as this intellectual, but he loved bundles. He loved pissing about. And Harauld and Mickie [Perch] loved the girls. Mickie was more flamboyant; he's been through more thatch than a roofer. Col went to accounting college at sixteen, so that didn't do him any favours in the ladies' department. Same face as Mickie, but totally different story. I did fine, had my moments, and so did 'Tiny' Clive. Girls could mother him. Just scoop him up. But Harauld and Mickie were the lads. Harauld had the voice, but Mickie had the barnet. He was the first person in the Elephant who managed to get his hair to be taller than his own head. Mickie always had three to four birds on the burner. He could only love in bulk. As opposed to the bulky, whom he couldn't love. But him and Harauld were careful to never fight over the same sort. That was honour. Once, Harauld took a shine to one of Mickie's birds and asked her to the pictures. Just that. And when Harauld and this bird came out, there we were in the lobby – Mickie, Me, Col and 'Tiny' Clive. And we all cut him with our eyes. We saw him, but we didn't look at him, if you know what I mean. And Harauld saw us not seeing him. He tried to lock eyes

20

with us, but we gave him icicles. He never forgot that day. And he never did it again. That became core: you don't go with another bloke's bird. Doesn't matter what you're doing or not doing, that's right out.

– But wasn't Hughes notorious for having affairs?

– Oh, it's obviously fine to have *affairs*. That's par for the course. Otherwise all you're left with is the wife. But you don't dip your toe in the neighbourhood pond. You don't take from your own.

– Hughes once said, 'Affairs require us to be honest, absolutely honest, in our deceptions.'

– I wouldn't go that far. You've got to cover your tracks.

– Right. So there's honour in dishonour?

– That's it.

– Do you think these questions of loyalty had a big effect on Hughes as a writer? His work is very bound up with betrayal, power and debt.

– Let me tell you something. Mickie went to prison, young, for a relatively minor theft. We were all bundling in this department store – by the sofas, said we were testing them – and just as we were bowling out, the bloke on the door got us by the collar: something had gone walkies, something silly – a fondue set, as it happens – and Mickie was fingered. Literally. The magistrate said that they needed to make an example of someone, and it might as well be Mickie. Mickie didn't even like cheese – it was too continental for him. He liked everything straight down the middle. Besides, who eats fondue in the summer? Colin was the one who went for cheese. He'd been to accounting college in Bury St Edmunds, so he'd been to King's Lynn, he'd been to Ely, he'd been to Bedford – he'd travelled all over. Colin loved it. For someone who looked like butter wouldn't melt in his mouth, he was obsessed with dairy. Mickie took the fall for Colin. But Mickie taking the fall meant that Colin owed him. And that's why Colin, instead of becoming the world-class accountant he could have been, ended up in Mickie's pocket for the rest of his life. Literally.

– Literally?

– Not literally. Figuratively. That's the one. Mickie would figuratively put you in his pocket. And, I suppose, Mickie was figuratively fingered. Col didn't want to run Mickie's businesses. But he had to. That's how Mickie related to you. He offered to do something for you, and he wouldn't take no for an answer, so you let him, and then you were his. It's why I won't get a Nando's loyalty card. Love your chicken, lads, but that don't mean you own me.

– So where are we now?

– I don't know – some kind of shit cafe.

– No, what year? Then. Not now. To avoid further . . .

– Well, we were fourteen, fifteen after the war. A year or so, and then Col went off to accounting college, that was three years – so 1950. That's when Mick did nick.

– Who's Nick?

– Stir . . .?

I hand him a teaspoon.

– Prison, you plank.

– Right. Sorry.

– That's when Mickie did time. Six months. Mickie said it was one of the happiest times of his life. He met all his future business partners in there. That's where he got all his contacts.

– Did Harauld ever consider university?

– No. University was for stiffs like Col. Eggheads. We wanted to be actors. We went to acting school. But we got chucked out after a couple of weeks.

– Any reason?

– Plenty. For a start, Harauld spoke so loudly he blew the teacher's toupee right off his bonce. And we drank a lot. That was when Mickie started setting up the clubs. We were permanently pie-eyed. We'd roll into class dribbling.

In 1951, Mickie Perch opened the nightclub Nice to Meat You, which became a feature of the post-war London 'scene'. Again, Mickie was the frontman, Colin cooked the books and Monkey cooked the all-meat menu. In 1952, the club was shut down by the police after someone found a human leg in the freezer. The team reunited with the sea-themed eatery Prawn Again, with its servers wearing shell bikinis, but that closed after an outbreak of cod worm. It was only when the Perch twins opened Mickie's, which combined all-day fry-ups, hard bop and topless waitresses, that they hit upon a winning formula. Because of the rules of public decency imposed by the Lord Chamberlain, the waitresses could be nude only if they were stationary, which meant that service was slow, but no one seemed to mind. Mickie's became *the* hang-out for sozzled jazzers, late-breakfasting showgirls and off-duty wrestlers. It was here that Donny Chapel, who would go on to provide the music for *O Bedlam! O Bedlam!*, developed his singular brand of socially committed skiffle. The club was a huge success, and the wealth generated would, in due course, help launch Hughes's career as a playwright.

— Did you know Harauld would become a playwright?

— I was the one who told him. I said, 'Harauld, how's about becoming a playwright?' He was never one for description, you know. He was a dialogue man. He was quick to pick up on how things were said, but if you asked him to describe, I don't know, a motor, he would barely know what colour it was. For Harauld, it was the intent. The motor is to get you from A to B. That's that. Who cares what it looks like? Harauld was a talker. That's not always the case with writers. With a lot of them, you hear them speak and you're like, 'I can see why you write.' But with Harauld, you heard him speak and you thought, 'Someone type this up.' Which is really what he did. A lot of those plays were things the boys had said. Things I'd said. Don't get me wrong, he knew *what* to type up. But often you'd hear a line and think, 'I've heard that before. That's something "Tiny" Clive said.'

— What led Mickie Perch to fund Hughes's first play, *Platform*?

— I think Harauld asked for an advance against what he was owed for working in the clubs. It was a little two-hander. The whole thing couldn't have cost more than four quid.

— But Mickie Perch was the producer?

— Yes. Technically. His name was on it. But Leslie organised it all.

— Leslie Francis? The director?

— What other Leslie Francis is there?

———————

Leslie Francis (1923–91) was a child of empire intent on seeing that empire fall. At sixteen he left school for Oxford University, where he studied Classics, English and Philosophy, an under-graduate course created especially for him. He interrupted his studies to work in the War Office, where he wrote many of Churchill's best jokes, but was dismissed when he criticised Churchill's delivery for being sentimental and lacking pace; Francis was reported to have said, 'Churchill may be winning the war, but he's killing my material.' He returned to Oxford and switched to Physics, in which he obtained a triple first, a grade created especially for him. He was asked to stay on for postgraduate work but had fallen under the spell of the cinema. 'I had a great sense that cinema needed wholesale reform, and how could I do that if I was mired in Further Physics?'

After some time working on various cinema periodicals and fanzines, Francis began his directorial career in industrial films and documentaries, the best known of which are *Hail to Thee, O Carrot!* (which won a Scottish BAFTA for Best New Non-Fiction Short in 1954), *Northern People* (1955), *As Far West as Wales* (1956) and *What Day's Wednesday?* (1957). He met Stoat and Hughes when he directed the science-fiction serial *Minions of the Moon* (1958), and again on the adventure series *Boudicca the Brave* (1955–9), in which Stoat starred as the titular marauder. Francis's television work, though in many respects unremarkable, was distinguished by the believability and naturalness of the acting.

Francis directed the long (61 mins) short *A Day Divided (Cannot Stand)* (1962), a fantasy set over the lunch hour of a factory worker in a Liverpool suburb, and the slight badminton drama *It's a Ruddy Racket!* (1964), but it was his film *And . . .?!* (1969), about a scout-group militia who attack the House of Lords, that would propel him into the first rank of cinematic greats.

As a theatre director, Francis had a long and fruitful collaboration with Hughes, starting in 1960 with *Platform* and ending with 1972's *Dependence*. He was also the director of *The Harauld Hughes Half-Hour Play*, overseeing the transposition of Hughes's writing to a new medium.

———————

— Was it a conscious decision to hide the fact that Harauld Hughes and Mickie Perch were half-brothers? I've been researching this period — the press releases, the interviews, etc. — but their being related is never mentioned.
— Mickie already had a rep. He wanted to be this larger-than-life impresario, so I think he didn't want anyone thinking that someone else could be on his level. That's why Col had to hide in the shadows. And I don't think Mickie wanted people thinking that he was, I don't know . . . soft. That he was putting his hand in his pocket to help his bookish little [half-]brother. And I think Harauld wanted to come across as his own man too. So they kept it to themselves.
— Did anyone know the truth?
— Those who knew, knew.
— And who were they?
— Those in the know.
— And who was that?
— Col, me, Monkey, 'Tiny' Clive. That was it.
— How did no one else guess? They grew up in the same house.
— Yeah, but they had different last names. They spoke differently. It was always separate. After the war everyone's houses were full of orphans. Fathers were thin on the ground.

- When you look at photos, though, the Perch twins and Hughes are virtually identical.
- People may have thought that, but they didn't say it because they didn't want to come across as being prejudiced. You know, no one wanted to say, 'Don't you two brown geezers look the same – you must be brothers?' Especially not to Mickie. He was pretty terrifying. And Mickie and Col were *actually* identical. So that acted as a kind of distraction. People didn't talk as much back then. I mean, if you didn't mention something, no one else mentioned it either.

It strikes me that Mick doesn't mention Felicity Stoat in relation to Harauld's formation as a playwright, even though she and Harauld had been married for seven years before *Platform* debuted on the London stage.

- When did Harauld meet Felicity Stoat?
- He was young. Too young maybe. They had a boy. Bartholomew. He had very bad IBS from birth. He was a case study. He's in all the medical books. He couldn't keep his grub down. Everything went straight through him.
- Did you admire Stoat as an actress?
- I *only* knew her as an actress. She didn't exactly take to our lot. She thought Mickie was vulgar. I mean, if you think wearing leopard print and back-combing your hair and carrying a stack of readies around is vulgar, then yes, he was vulgar. But once she and Harauld got hitched, Harauld left the group. It's like he became a different person. We wouldn't see him down Mickie's no more; he became very inward. I mean, get married – do what you like – but don't let it affect your life. And then, to cap it all, he moved out of the Elephant.

– Where to?

– Fucking Chiswick, if you can believe that. Said the Elephant wasn't a place to bring up a boy. I said, 'That's where we grew up,' and he said, 'I rest my case.' He wanted somewhere leafy. I said trees don't confer some kind of moral probity. They don't make you better. I said, 'What the hell are you going to do in Chiswick? You might as well move to the country. You'll be out of it. You can't live in Chiswick and *act*, they're a contradiction in terms.'

– Could one say that it was Stoat who, by encouraging Hughes to withdraw from a life of nightclubs and bundling, made him a writer?

– She made him a houseboy. That's what she did. He worked for her. He would've been a writer whether he'd met her or not. And, by the way, that story about the two of them meeting on a train platform is pure bollocks. She was the one who spread that about.

———————

In *Herstory*, Lady Lovilocke challenges the 'silly myth' of Stoat and Hughes's platform meet-cute. According to her, Hughes and Stoat met when they were both actors on *Minions of the Moon*, though their encounter was not on the lunar surface; it was in the voice booth, after Stoat was summoned, as per her contract, to record additional dialogue. Hardly a perfectionist, nor able to self-correct, Stoat's speech often hovered close to the limits of intelligibility, even by the standards of television. Harauld provided the voice for the opinionated robot butler, Peevron 3000 (shortened to P3K and then, finally, 'P'), a droid whose emotional circuits had been damaged in transit. P3K is a jolly good butler, but is verbally abusive, often to comic effect. Harauld had great fun with the character and frequently stood the sound engineer a pint or two of stout in the pub after his regular recording sessions. And it was at one such session that he first encountered Stoat. Lovilocke describes it in her memoir:

Felicity, unable to exempt herself from any gathering for fear that others might manage to live on in her absence, invited herself along for the post-recording libation. She became obsessed with Harauld and pursued him relentlessly. On set, she began fluffing her lines with abandon so that she could spend more and more time in the booth.

Harauld, ever the romantic, and yet to realise the devastating effect of his good looks, was defenceless. Before long, Felicity was with child, and a marriage was hastily arranged, tying Harauld down with the premature strings of domesticity at a time when he should have been taking full advantage of his nascent virility. Must we wonder at the anger expressed by those prowling men in Harauld's early plays? How could anyone be content, living cheek by jowl in woeful kitchen diners, their ceilings farcically low, and no home library or study to which one could retire, let alone a games room? Harauld's early adulthood was a dense thicket of frustration, while his wife, dripping with the water from Narcissus's pool, swanned off through the glade, leaving him to hold the baby, often literally, while she fronted one ghastly TV serial after another.

Mick continues:

— With Stoaty on the up-and-up, Harauld had to keep his aspirations in abeyance. A man of his calibre could have been playing lead roles, but Felicity was the priority – she was the bigger star. Harauld ended up being the sole carer for their son. And Bartholomew was a nightmare from the get-go. He would cry and cry unless you picked him up. And he went through more milk than a custard factory. He was like a sieve. Felicity said she wouldn't give him the tit because she thought it would ruin her figure. I think it's because that little shit would've sucked her dry.

———————

When Hughes was cast as an intergalactic bishop in *Space Church*, a series about the fate of a motley crew of intergalactic evangelists facing an ecumenical schism, he asked if his character could be a single father so that he could continue to feed Bartholomew his warm milk on set. Leslie Francis agreed to cast Bartholomew as 'Space Urchin' and added luminous dye to his bottled milk to make it look more futuristic. The dye may have contributed to the worsening of Bartholomew's various gastric complaints.

Later, I ask Dan Director if we might be able to locate a clip of *Space Church*, but he tells me it has been 'sadly wiped', before adding, 'That's what they should call a care home for old television actors. Sadly Wiped. Get it?' I tell him I do get it but that I'm not a good laugher.

———————

- You acted opposite Felicity Stoat in six Hughes plays: *Platform*, *Table*, *Roost*, *Roast*, *Flight* and *Dependence*.
- You asking me or telling me?
- How was her working relationship with Hughes?
- There's work, and there's the relationship. I only know about the work.

— But you said you and Hughes were extremely close.
— I never said we were close, I said we were tight.
— Is that different from being close?
— It's a different word.
— I'm sensing this is difficult territory.
— Known for your empathy, are you?

I can't help but detect a Hughesian tone to our exchange. In *Roast*, Barrett was the original 'Pete'.

                    CHARLIE
          And whence do these clues emanate?

                         PETE
          Whence? What's whence?

                    CHARLIE
          Whence. 'From where'.

                         PETE
          Then why don't you say 'from where'?

                    CHARLIE
          Because 'whence' is shorter. 'Whence'
          is the contraction.

                         PETE
          Well, it's not contracted this
          exchange, has it, mate? It's made it
          longer. It's dragged the arse out of
          it.

— Did Hughes write with Felicity Stoat in mind?
— I think he tried to get her out of his mind. That's why he
wrote so much while he was married. Anyway, I shouldn't
speak ill of the dead. Stoat wanted Harauld to write.
Without Harauld she wouldn't have worked. She didn't care
about him; she cared about what he could do and who he
was.

31

- I don't feel you've quite answered the question about her as an actress.
- Have you seen *Boudicca the Brave*? All she did was slap her thigh and shout the word 'Ha!' If she was such a star, how come she was never in anything after that, apart from what Harauld wrote. Answer me that.
- I understand she drank?
- We all drank. Acting *is* drinking. You get rid of drink, you get rid of actors. That's what they've done now. These days, all they drink is smoothies. They're all so beefy. It's disgusting. They don't have faces. None of the actors these days have a face you could feel anything for, except a kind of hatred. I look at these faces now and all I think is, 'Fuck me, you look healthy.' There's no excess. All their personality's gone into their biceps. It's the end.
- Did you ever bear a grudge about the fact that you tended to lose out on the roles you created on stage when they were translated to the screen? I suppose I'm thinking of *The Harauld Hughes Half-Hour Play*.
- I was always grateful to Harauld. Leslie [Francis] said to me, 'Mick, there are some people whom the camera loves. And you aren't one of them.' Harauld hated the way he looked on camera too. It made him sweat. Just point a camera at Harauld, and he started to drip like meat on a radiator. I'm a stage actor. My eyes are set very far back in my head. It's hard to get any light to them – they look like the opposite end of a tunnel. The only thing that works is light from below, which is fine on stage – that's what footlights are for – but on screen I look like Boris Karloff. And no one wants to look like Boris Karloff. Even Boris Karloff didn't want to look like Boris Karloff.

– So how did you feel when Hughes started to turn his attention to writing screenplays?

– Well, that did me no favours. It was good for Mickie and it was good for Colin in a way. I mean, they made a fortune, cos they produced the films. But I think it was the end for Harauld, really. That's what did for him. But he owed Mickie, so that was that.

– How did he owe Mickie?

– I suggest you ask Mickie.

Barrett has turned rueful and lights a cigarette. No one has the heart to admonish him, but the cafe owner emits a cough of sufficient theatricality that Wiggsy Sound raises his arm for quiet.

– In the early days, we swore we would die for the right part, for the right play, for the right words. Those plays are magic. They're alive. But Mickie [Perch] didn't care for the theatre. So Harauld ends up in B pictures and ads. And for what? Money. I may not have money, but I have my pride.

I wonder whether Mick Barrett will use some of that pride to pay for his second 'Cooked 3'.

– Did you watch the films when they came out?

– Course I did. Harauld was my boy. I told him what I thought.

– What did you think?

– Not much.

– Of the films or in general?

– I liked Ibssen well enough. He had an eye.

33

– Ibssen Anderssen directed all of Hughes's scripts bar
  O Bedlam! O Bedlam!
– I know. Why are you telling me?
– I'm saying it for the benefit of the audience, I suppose.
– That's the problem with film. It's all for the benefit of the
  audience. The people making them get paid, but do they
  really benefit?

The Norwegian director Ibssen Anderssen died, unexpectedly,
at the age of thirty-six. Much later, on the fifth anniversary of
his death, he was remembered in a tabloid article entitled 'You
Made Me Dizzy, Mr Ibby!', which featured selected eulogies
from some of the women in his life.

BY FELICITY STOAT
star of *The Swinging Models*

Between 1966 and 1974, Ibssen Anderssen directed seven of
the most impactful, outré and downright subversive films ever
to have been made on UK soil. Critics have tended to divide
them into two trilogies, while ignoring *The Glowing Wrong*,
a film from which Anderssen was fired. Literally, if one is to
believe certain rumours (and I *do* believe them . . .).

Ibssen was an artist, and his medium was the cinema. He
never claimed to be a writer, though he undoubtedly made
contributions to the scripts of each of the films he made. He
was also my lover and perhaps the kindest man I've ever met.
I was once married to a man who is still considered to be one
of the most important playwrights since the war. It's certainly
true that the best of him is on the page. Once, in what he
called 'a perfectly reasonable fit of anguish' (in other words,

a tantrum), he bashed his head against the bedhead so hard he completely blacked out. When he came round, his only concern was whether he had somehow knocked all the unwritten plays out of his head. 'Don't worry,' I said. 'Sh*t sticks.'

Ibby was different. The connection between us was electric, like a cable. And the results showed on screen. He knew how to photograph women – he looked at you as if you were a goddess. 'You are my shining star,' he would say. Harauld would never have used such clichéd language. He wouldn't tell me what he thought. He would go away and write a bloody poem. Well, nothing turns off a girl quicker than someone reciting their own blank verse. Ibssen would never write a poem. He *was* a poem. For him, the screenplay was simply a means to an end – something that meant he could photograph people. Actual flesh-and-blood people. Not abstractions. Not something as silly as words.

BY INGER MARIE
star of *The Terrible Witch*

Ibssen Anderssen was a rock star. The directors before him, they were like your dad – they all smoked pipes and wore eyepatches and looked like their spit would be brown. Ibby was the first director whom girls *liked*. Why is it that beautiful women want to be around men who are always around beautiful women? I think it's that women want to be desired. And Ibby was full of desire. He was an *expert* in desire. He wanted his girlfriends to look just so. He chose the clothes, the make-up, the hair. He *created* you. He was *Pygmalion* on acid.

BY DINKI GUSTAVSON
star of *The Awful Woman in Space*

I didn't like Ibby. He was always trying to pressure me into threesomes. He kept saying how they were a very natural and beautiful thing and I should stop being so uptight and not cool. And then I said, 'Okay – what about you, me and another guy?' And that made him very angry and he told me I should be ashamed of myself. He was a child, a child stuffing himself and trying to get as many of his nerve endings tingling as he could. But I'd say that Harauld was no better – it's just that his high was language. He was obsessed with pushing words around a page. What about people? Don't people come before language?

– But despite your reservations regarding the form, you still appeared in some of the [Anderssen/Hughes] films.
– I know.
– But in smaller roles than one would perhaps expect.
– I should have played 'Ian' in *The Swinging Models*. It would have been twice the film. But Mickie wanted to be in the movies. Terrible actor.
– But you did get to play a photographer in *The Especially Wayward Girl*.
– The part didn't even have a name. I was billed as 'Photographer'. I had about four lines in the whole thing. It was just a bit of bread. As Harauld once said to me, 'You can't feed yourself on the begrudging esteem of your peers.'
– There are lines that you say that seem almost ironically literal. For example: 'That's a wrap on today's photographing. Thanks for all those groovy poses.'
– I just say the lines. I mean, I wouldn't normally say, 'It's this wind. It drives everyone crazy.' But that's what was written.
– You played 'Police Officer' in *The Deadly Gust*.
– There's a story to go with that line.
– Great. Perhaps you could tell it.

– Course I'm going to tell it. I'm not just going to say, 'Here's a great story,' and then shut up shop, am I? Right. Where was I?

– A story about *The Deadly Gust*?

– You've lost me.

– To do with the line you had?

– What line?

– 'It's this wind. It drives everyone crazy.'

– That's it. And we'll put that little diversion under the heading 'The Perils of Interrupting'. Anyway, Harauld was always on set. Because he wanted every line to be said just so. Just as he wrote it. Even if it was a typo. I thought it would give it a bit more of an edge if I said, 'It's this *fucking* wind, it drives everyone crazy.' So I just lob it in. I say it. I give it a go. And I hear Harauld, not Ibssen, scream, 'Cut!' And he storms over and says – you know the voice – 'I think you have misunderstood the line, Mick. It's "this wind", not "this fucking wind". Wind doesn't fuck.' I said, 'You haven't been to Newcastle.' Which didn't make sense, but it still made us laugh.

———————

The following is from *Herstory* by Lady Lovilocke:

I have had seven or eight Norwegian lovers, many of them sea captains, and they were wonderfully undemanding – you would barely know they were there but for the faint, and not disagreeable, smell of brine. Norwegians keep themselves to themselves and rarely offer an opinion. They are quiet, accepting and physically indefatigable. Such a character must have been of great value to Harauld, who could rage like the

North Sea and needed a robust harbour that could brook the typhoons that are apt to accompany creation. I can still picture the bubbling froth at the sides of Harauld's mouth, globular souvenirs of invective that would migrate onto his lower lip and catch magically in the light before dripping onto his pulsing neck. You had to be strong during these tempests. Ibssen was like a mighty spruce. He would bend in the wind, but he would not fall. Harauld needed to turn words over in his mouth, to see how they tasted, to see if they had texture. Ibssen was happy to wait. He had all the time in the world. Ibssen never gave Harauld a note, he never asked questions, he didn't interfere. Ibssen was the perfect collaborator.

———————

— How was Ibssen Anderssen on set?
— He was the director, where else would he be?
— I meant more, what was he like?
— What's anyone like? He was Norwegian. You know Norwegians.
— My mother was Norwegian.
— Well, there you go. Ibssen didn't say much. He just shot the film, you know? He loved his spliff, his uppers, his ludes, and he always had some dreamy-looking bird hanging around. That was Ibssen. Totally different story with Leslie [Francis]. I was a Leslie man. Leslie *directed*. Ibssen *photographed*. Leslie believed in the intention being clear. Even if it was surreal, it had to be grounded in some kind of meaning. Hughes would never talk about meaning. It just *was*. I think that's what the problem was when those two [Hughes and Francis on *Bedlam*] tried to do a film together. They hadn't worked out how to create something in tandem.

They wasn't even day and night – it was all night. But on stage, in the theatre, when it was me and Leslie, working out how to do Harauld, we were the nuts. The unbeatable nuts.

– I wish I could have seen some of those original productions.

– They're gone. Fleeting. Like all great theatre. Film is something else. It's a magic trick. It can impress you, but only if you don't know how it works.

– Don't you think film can be art?

– Not from what I've seen . . .

– But it reaches more people though?

– More people would see Harauld telling a silly story on a chat show than ever saw his plays. Reach, my arse. But once he got a sniff of that reach, why bother? Why go to the blank page and have your heart smashed out on it when you can just wing it?

– I wonder whether he stopped writing when he met Lady Lovilocke because he became healed in a way; he didn't have to exorcise all this pain.

– You know, round about the time he stopped, Harauld began to appear in an ad for an insurance company. 'You handle the drama, we'll handle the insurance' – that's how it went. He became rich. Or, as is the case with becoming rich, not quite rich enough. So he kept doing the ads, and he kept doing the chat shows, and he kept talking about his work to people who wished he would work again but were too afraid to tell him that because he was Harauld Hughes.

– What did you tell him?

– I told him to write a play. He said he was trying. I didn't see him as frequently as in the old days, but he always kept in touch. Christmas. Birthdays. And he'd always stand you a pint. I was in Harauld's first-ever play, and I was in his last. And of that, at least, I'm proud. And also, to some extent, my children.

— What do you think about the fact that more people have come to know the Hughesian pause from the way he timed the gap between 'You handle the drama' and 'we'll handle the insurance' than from anything he wrote himself?

Mick doesn't answer; he has five slices of fried bread in him and is starting to slow down. There's so much more I want to ask him — about rehearsing with Francis, about the themes in Hughes's work — but Dan is making the 'wrap it up' motion.

— Did Hughes ever talk about *O Bedlam! O Bedlam!*?
— Harauld didn't talk to anyone about that. It's not the kind of thing anyone likes to talk about.
— Would you mind answering that again, but putting the question in the answer?
— Yes, I would. I would mind that very fucking much.
— Because this documentary is called *The Unfinished Harauld Hughes*, so we're trying to dig down into the works he didn't complete. And *Bedlam* is the big one.
— That sounds like your problem. Not mine.

There is a long pause. A Hughesian one.

— I would say good luck, Mick continues, but I think the whole thing should just be left to rot.

When Dan yells, 'Cut!' Barrett, by instinct, picks up his yolk-coated knife and presses it to my throat.

Harauld Hughes, Mickie Perch and Ibssen Anderssen made seven features together for The Anglers Production Company (Colin Perch, though involved in the financing, never took an on-screen credit). The combination of the Perch brothers' business acumen, Anderssen's photographic facility and the solidity of Hughes's screenplays meant shooting proceeded very smoothly, and seldom with more than two takes. The results were both spectacular and inexpensive, the golden mean of cinema in any genre. They were niche films, granted, but well regarded, particularly in underground circles.

Mickie Perch was an advocate of what he called 'Adultainment', and theatre was far from what he thought that word meant. 'I don't understand why they're pretending we can't see them,' Perch reportedly said, though perhaps not at a Brecht revival.

'Until they work out how to blow things up on stage, theatre will always come second to cinema. I like motion,' he said. 'Motion is lotion for the soul. Whether it's making love, delivering a roundhouse to someone's throat or tracking down a creditor, it feeds the spirit. And the maximum motion you can have is an explosion.' Perch demanded his films have 'good-looking girls, kung fu, chase scenes and humour', insisting that there was no tension between being a champion of women and an 'ardent appreciator of the unrobed female form'.

But once Hughes started adapting these films from their outlandish sources, with their absurd monsters and circular narratives, it seems, to me at least, that he couldn't prevent himself from complexifying and deepening the dramaturgy. Hughes couldn't create stock genre 'types'; he could only create characters. He is the opposite of Ian, the jaundiced photographer in *The Swinging Models*, casually rebuking his latest conquest, Solveig . . .

> IAN
> A model isn't a woman. A model is a
> type of woman. The ideal type. And
> I decide what that ideal type is.
> Me. Ian. If you conform to the ideal
> type, then you get paid. And if you
> don't, well, you've got no business
> being a model.

. . . but Hughes, that staunch defender of the undefended, demands Solveig's individuation. She breaks away from Ian and Celeste (played by Felicity Stoat), the sadistic manager of the model agency Celeste's, and becomes an actress, an actress about to make her debut in an exciting new SF film. As she tells us in breathless voice-over:

> SOLVEIG
> I used to be a model, and I'm still a
> model with a lovely face. Only now I'm
> an actress too, and a damn good one. I
> can walk through any door I want.

Contrast that to the end of Hughes's television play *Prompt*, in which an actor, trapped in a single spotlight, stands, forced to confess his corruption, his moral bankruptcy, to reveal his performance as counterfeit:

> [The Actor] looks at the footlights.
>   Constance is crouching, pen in hand,
> looking up from the script.
>   She whispers.
>   CONSTANCE
> Tell them you're a fraud.

42

The Actor looks at her, beseeching, his
eyes widening.
  She echoes his look.
  He looks back at her. It becomes clear
that she is not going to feed him the
lines.

                    THE ACTOR
I'm a fraud.

                    CONSTANCE
'And I am in a fraudulent play.'

                    THE ACTOR
And I am in a fraudulent play.

                    CONSTANCE
'Directed by a fraudulent man.'

The Actor looks to the side. Leslie is in
a rictus of fury. The Actor looks back
to Constance. She is applying lipstick,
checking the results by looking in a
hand-held mirror.

                    THE ACTOR
Directed by a fraudulent man.

                    CONSTANCE
'Produced by a man who hasn't even read
it.'

                    THE ACTOR
Produced by a man who hasn't even read
it.

                    CONSTANCE
'Because he too is a fraud.'

                    THE ACTOR
Because he too is a fraud.

Powerful? Of course. Uplifting? Not so much. Could it be
that Hughes felt a greater compassion for the characters in his
adapted work? I rather wonder whether he pitied them for being
born into such crass settings and, as a result, sought to ennoble

them, bestowing upon them a heroic bearing that he would never allow *his* creations, birthed in unforgiving landscapes of his own making. In short: he was much harder on his own children.

As much as I admire Hughes's plays, their compression, their ellipses, their verbal savagery, my heart always leaps when I see the following credit appear:

An Anglers Production

Directed by Ibssen Anderssen
Screenplay by Harauld Hughes
Produced by Mickie Perch

There is something trinitarian about the shared card, its purported division of labour speaking of a much deeper indivisibility evoked in Freud's psychological model. Perch is the id, the pure pleasure principle; Hughes is the ego, translating those impulses into something comprehensible, a narrative; the civilising force of the superego (in this configuration) fell to Ibssen Anderssen, who situated the work in the shared semiotics of film. The image.

But Hughes was always in the middle. In Augustus Pink's biography of him, he quotes Hughes:

The Anglers wouldn't have existed without Mickie. Mickie was the catalyst. He was the guy who said, 'Let's rip up the rule book.' Mickie hated rules. And books. So, as you can imagine, a rule book was his worst nightmare. Colin was all rules. Ibssen was all flair. I held the centre. I *was* the bloody centre.

But Hughes, a man immodest enough to admit that he knew, from an early age, that his name 'would become adjectival', often struggled to evince pride in his film work. He once said:

44

When all civilisation is as dust and becomes silt at the bottom of a chemical sea, the memories that remain will be of those brave enough to continue writing for the theatre. The stage is a battleground, and one gets to replay the same battle over and over, to reach for a greater understanding that, at its best, is as close to glory as one can hope for on this blasted earth. Film is a playground, a ride that's meant to take you from a state of expectation, through a series of safely exhilarating twists and turns, to a state of satiation. It is the ultimate capitalist art form. It's story as service industry. It's a totally separate type of writing. It's just like using another muscle.

But there's no use denying the impact screenwriting had on Hughes's playwrighting, as this timeline attests (note: stage plays appear in CAPITALS; films/televised plays are in *italics*):

1960 – PLATFORM, directed by Leslie Francis, opens in the West End. The producer is Mickie Perch, though he is not involved artistically. The play receives poor notices and loses money. Harauld signs a ten-picture contract with The Anglers Production Company (which Mickie runs with Colin) to offset some of the incurred loss. The accounting for this 'Recoupment' is entirely at Mickie's discretion.

1961 – TABLE opens in Guildford. It is a modest success but doesn't transfer.

1962 – ROAST and ROOST open at the Royal Court. The plays run for the rest of the year.

Hughes and Stoat move into a grand six-storey house in St John's Wood. The property is owned by Mickie Perch and rented to Hughes and Stoat in lieu of Perch's continued support for Hughes's theatrical endeavours. Perch regrets to inform Hughes that because of the high cost of the property, The Recoupment will have to be deferred until Hughes can

45

afford to buy the property outright, which is not possible because the house is not for sale.

1963 – Hughes is contracted to do uncredited script 'doctoring' on *It's a Ruddy Racket!*, directed by Leslie Francis. The film is critically acclaimed, though Hughes's (low) fee goes towards The Recoupment.

1964 – FLIGHT opens in the West End and cements Hughes's move away from the Royal Court. It is not a financial success. The Recoupment starts to accrue interest. In desperation, Hughes allows Perch to pitch a TV adaptation of his theatrical works.

1965 – *The Harauld Hughes Half-Hour Play* debuts on British television. Owing to a national transport strike that leaves people stranded at home, the first episode, *Platform*, is seen by nearly half the country. The series receives wide acclaim, and Hughes becomes a publicly recognised figure. Hughes writes two new television-only plays, *Prompt* and the shorter piece *Shunt*.

1966 – *The Swinging Models*, scripted by Hughes, directed by Ibssen Anderssen and produced by Mickie Perch, is released and becomes a 'hit'. It is notable for being the first English film to feature a woman saying the word 'shit'. Despite the revenues generated, Hughes's share of the profits is negligible and entirely swallowed up by The Recoupment.

1967 – *The Especially Wayward Girl*, scripted by Hughes, is another collaboration with Anderssen and Perch. It does less well than *The Swinging Models*, but still makes a healthy profit. An 'unforeseen tax burden' means that Mickie Perch has to freeze any possibility of reducing The Recoupment for another seven years.

1968 – *The Model and the Rocker* completes *The Models Trilogy*. It is a commercial success, though a plateau, artistically.

1969 – *The Terrible Witch* is released. It starts a cycle of rip-off films, including *The Even More Terrible Witch* and *Son of a Witch*, to which Hughes contributes uncredited material.

1970 – *The Awful Woman from Space* sees Hughes explore a new milieu, 'soft SF'.

1971 – Hughes works on the screenplay for *Harlem Shuttle*, about an inner-city badminton team. The film is not made.

1972 – Hughes writes DEPENDENCE. He receives an honour for creating the Year's Longest Play in Proportion to Its Script. *The Times* describes it as 'more pause than play' and 'spectacularly hermetic'. It is his last work for the stage.

Harauld Hughes went from seven plays in six years, before his first film, to writing one play in eight. Between 1973 and 1976, he would write *The Deadly Gust*, *The Glowing Wrong* and, finally, *O Bedlam! O Bedlam!*, which, to all intents and purposes, marks the end of Hughes.

What happened?

3

HERSTORY

                    HE
        Well, I can't speak to your
        feelings.

                    SHE
        To what are you speaking,
        if not my feelings?

            From *Table* (1961) by Harauld Hughes,
                published by Faber & Faber

Dan has hired an actress to play the young Lady Virginia
Lovilocke. Extracts from her book *Herstory* are to be 'peppered
throughout the piece'. I ask Dan why can't we ask the real Lady
Lovilocke to read from it herself?

  – We've only got her ladyship for an hour, max. And she's
    probably pretty juddery by now. She's got to be late eighties.
  – And has she approved this?
  – What do you mean, 'this'?
  – Someone playing her?
  – Why would I need her permission?
  – Courtesy?
  – Who are you? Sir Lancelot? Get over yourself, mate – it's
    not as if anyone owns their life story.
  – But you can, and do, own your own book of your life story.
  – We're basically promoting it. She should be paying us.
    Someone might even buy her book.

49

There is no heating in our abandoned office block; the walls are angry with bubbling mould. The actress is seated against a burnt-orange backdrop designed to evoke 'fading memory'. To her right, just beyond her reminiscences, lies a heap of silty office chairs and a water fountain in the foetal position. A pigeon protests in the light well. Dan beckons me away from the camera.

– Do you think she looks haughty enough?

We are standing by a monitor at the opposite end of the room, next to a whiteboard on which are written the words 'Always be solutioning'.

– Can she hear us?
– I hope not.

I drop my voice to an accusatory hiss.

– What do you mean, 'haughty'?
– I asked the casting lady for someone who had that posh, haughty look.

Dan has maintained the same speaking volume.

– You *asked* for someone with a posh, haughty look?
– What would you have asked for?
– Not that.
– I think I also said cruel-looking. But in an attractive way. Like, 'You are so far below me you're like a worm to me.'
– You find that attractive?
– Doesn't everyone?

He bounds over to Tony Camera and, even though no one is talking, loudly calls for silence.

Dust motes dance round the tendrils of the actress's beehive. I say 'actress' not just because I don't know her name, but because there is something apposite about using that depersonalised designation – the same abstract mononym used for Felicity Stoat's character in *Platform*.

Hughes's marriage to Stoat, which lasted from 1953 until its official dissolution in 1980, was unhappy, distant, but creatively productive; his marriage to Lady Lovilocke was happy, close and seemed to put his creativity into endless abeyance. Stoat never wrote her life story, but Lady Lovilocke did. Our actress leans forward to tell it.

CAPTION: '1965'

The first time I saw Harauld, we were in different rooms. I was at a girlfriend's house in Chelsea. She had taken delivery of a rather handsome new television set and wanted to give it a spin. A few of the old crowd had gathered for cocktails, along with some new faces, all illustrious, all attractive and very much part of the London 'scene'. I remember one of our number excitedly informing me that she'd just been to bed with one of The Beatles, she couldn't remember which one, and proceeded to do a terribly funny impression of his accent. I knew The Beatles because I was having an affair with a prominent pop photographer, or I thought I was, until I turned around and saw him enjoying a prolonged snog with a narrow model with long legs and jet-black hair, her miniskirt made micro as it caught on the velvet sofa. 'Well, that's a bust,' I thought, as his hungry hand spidered up her thigh, 'but I suppose that's men for you!'

As those assembled started to pair off
and retire to various rooms, I realised I
was alone, with only this new device for
company. Could anything be more appalling?
Drinking wine in front of the television!
That's when I saw a man appear on the
screen. Or rather, I heard a man from
the screen, for I had dozed off, and it
was a deep, urgent voice that had roused
me. My Chablis had puddled around my own
leg. Affronted, in a dreamy sort of way,
I looked around for a napkin or anything
low-value and absorbent. But the voice
stopped me from looking for very long. It
contained such potency, such poignancy,
that I had to see from whence it came.
Surely it would be a large, barrel-chested
man, a dishy scrum forward of some kind.
But no. The man was tall but slim, with a
bookish manner and fierce black eyes. He
was wearing a black jacket and a perfectly
awful polo neck that made it look like he
had no throat. He was standing on a black
stage, lit only by a single spotlight.
There were a few beads of sweat on his
forehead; they danced near a tight throng
of veins. He had a gap between his two
front teeth and spat rather a lot as he
spoke. He was presenting a short play of
his called *Platform*, one of a series that
featured in his very own show, entitled
The Harauld Hughes Half-Hour Play.
   Even when a mostly naked man walked into
the room, in search of a sustaining slice
of toast, I barely apprehended him. 'Would
you like some?' he asked. 'Yes, please,'
I'm told I replied, before drifting back
to sleep. But I wasn't talking about the
toast, and I wasn't talking about the man
who had offered to make me some. I was
talking about the man on the television.
That man, of course, was Harauld Hughes.
As I slept, I dreamed of him and hoped to
be transported to that spotlight, for us

to feel the heat of the arc lamp on us
both. I had, in fact, fallen asleep rather
close to an actual lamp, and this time it
was the smell of my hair burning that woke
me up. I bunged my head under the tap and
headed straight out to the King's Road to
buy a television. I must have looked a
fright when I brought it home. My husband,
Langley, was appalled. 'What will we do
with it?' he said. He didn't notice that
I'd had to cut off all my hair.

***

The next time I saw Harauld was six years
later, at a poetry recital in honour of
some of the poems T. S. Eliot thought
of writing, but ultimately decided not
to. Harauld had a protracted physical
altercation with a latecomer that ended
with the man losing some of his thumb. In
fact, the man's cries can be heard on the
vinyl recording of the event. Fortunately,
my father was a viscount, and he helped
Harauld settle the matter privately. The
event certainly brought Harauld and I to
one another's attention, but we were both
married and already in the middle of other
affairs. But the pull between us was to
prove irresistible.

'1971'

October 12th
Finally met Harauld Hughes. He's even
louder in person, and rather more handsome.
His teeth aren't as bad as they look on
television, and they're more yellow than
black, even though he smokes like a bloody
rocket. He gave me a volume of his own
poetry. I didn't recognise the publisher.
He said it was a limited-edition private
pressing. I asked him why he didn't get it
published properly. I hope he didn't take

it as a slight. Nevertheless, he wrote a touching inscription: 'To Virginia. From Harauld.' 'Will you read it?' he asked. I said I would. 'How will I find out what you thought?' But I could feel Langley at my elbow and said I had to go. On the way back with L in the car, I couldn't stop thinking about H. He'd looked at me with such ferocity that it was either ardour or derision. I can't decide which. I dare say I don't care as long as he's thinking of me.

***

Over the years, many people have told me that they're convinced Harauld hated them. When I ask where they got that idea from, they say that it's something to do with the way he looked at them. I tell them not to worry; that, at first, Harauld looks at everyone like they're an ant. I once asked Harauld why he had to look so intensely at people, as if they were insects. 'But I like insects!' he said.

'1976'

Five years later, Harauld was competing in a charity badminton tournament to raise funds for one of those terrible conflicts that kept springing up in Africa, and he asked me to join him for the mixed doubles. My children were terribly upset, of course, because they were home from school that Saturday, and after that I would be in Europe for the rest of the year, but I found myself saying yes to Harauld and, in a sense, to the rest of my life.

February 19th
Played badminton with Harauld Hughes. He's terrifically good, though he said he was off his game. I was so 'beguiling' that he couldn't concentrate! Or so he claimed.

He asked me what I thought of his poems. I
said, 'I'm here, aren't I?' 'Yes, you are,'
he said. Had a drink at the players' bar
afterwards. Harauld has his own key so he
can lock up. It was 3 a.m. by the time his
driver took us [to Lady Lovilocke's] home
in his Bentley. Langley away somewhere,
possibly Scotland, children asleep on the
top floor. Invited Harauld in for coffee
(as long as he promised to be quiet),
and we drank champagne from china cups.
He wasn't quiet, and when the children
woke up, he played tag with them. Haven't
laughed so much in years. He left at around
7 a.m. Later, he calls me to say he has
run all the way home, his driver trundling
behind. 'Where's home?' I ask. 'With you.
If you'll have me.' How can I resist?

* * *

Why would I risk my life? All that I had
built up? I was the proverbial 'woman who
had it all': an aristocratic title, an
idyllic estate, beautiful horses, eight
or nine wonderful children, a thriving
career within the confines of the time
and a wealthy older husband with deep
pockets and rapidly declining health. I'd
met men before, some I'd even taken to
bed, just as I presumed my husband, Lord
Langley Lovilocke, had had his adventures
as a highly decorated submarine commander
during the war, but none of these men had
meant much, at least not to me. They were
just a bit of fizz.
   I enjoyed being wooed and made love to,
especially if the suitor was handsome, yet
the physical aspect was rarely important
to me (though men seem to consider it
so terribly pressing) and I find that
if one can find a way to let them just
get on with it, they do become much more
relaxed and agreeable company. Until I met

55

Harauld, I never saw what all the fuss was about, by which I mean, I suppose, sex. Yet these lovers of mine all seemed so terribly keen on it, and it never took too long, so I was perfectly happy to oblige. I've always felt the urge to please, and afterwards they looked rather sweet as they slept, all puffed out and proud of the pleasure of which they believed themselves to be the sole cause.

But Harauld was different. He didn't sleep afterwards. He wanted to talk. He had so much to say. I wonder if there has ever been anyone with as much to say as Harauld. And I loved to hear him speak. How could I not, with that wonderful baritone of his? And those sparkling black eyes, shining with his indefatigable sense of enquiry, that relentless capacity for play?

Harauld had got it into his head that we were destined to be together and that he couldn't live without me, which was so terribly touching. Even had he not made such attestations of ardour, it was clear, even to me, that I had no intention of resisting Harauld. I admired my husband enormously, but he was much older than I was, older even than my own father and, if anything, even more distant. Langley was happiest on his submarine, surrounded by all those chaps, though he wouldn't tolerate any behaviour that he deemed 'fey' or 'queen-y', especially underwater. He simply disliked the pressure of one-on-one intimacy. He would become agitated if the house had fewer than a dozen people in it. I often wonder whether that's why he wanted so many children, just to keep the head count up at the dining-room table. Even when we made love, he had to listen to the World Service.

'You have the measure of me,' Harauld once told me. We were still in the first flush of romance, and we were having

oysters and Scotch at Le Caprice. 'You're
the only attractive woman I've met who
I couldn't crush intellectually.' 'It's
not "who", Harauld, it's "whom",' I
said, and shucked an oyster with no
little elan. He stood up and shouted, 'I
love this pedantic woman!' I could have
died. But I didn't. Tom Stoppard stood
up and led a round of applause. So much
for keeping things a secret. I had the
measure of Langley too, I suppose, but the
measurement had started to come up short.
It wasn't his fault; it was entirely mine.
I never could stand to be bored.

'You're no pushover,' Harauld would
say to me. Which I always found strange,
because Harauld never wanted to push me
over. He held me up. Perhaps that's why
we stayed together for so long. Very
quickly, I came to lean on him, and if
he left me, I knew I would fall. Once I
went on the London underground to see what
it was like. It made such a thundering
sound, and it was so interesting to look
at everyone, locked in their worlds, with
such distress clouding their faces, their
worries of lives unlived, each unable
to see how beautiful Creation truly is.
Still, the carriage was packed, and I
didn't want to spoil my new dress by
sitting down, so I stood close to the
door. I was pressed right up against it,
the smell was dreadful, and when the Tube
finally arrived at South Ken, the doors
opened without warning, and I tumbled out,
unable to support myself, and fell into
a heap on the ground. Well, that's how I
felt when Harauld died.

When Tony Camera lifts his head from the eyepiece, he looks
like he's been crying, but he reassures us that it's something to
do with the dust.

57

It is tempting to speculate as to what would have occurred if Hughes had simply asked for Lord Lovilocke's understanding, rather than for him to set Lady Lovilocke free. I wonder whether Lord Lovilocke would have accepted, so long as Hughes and Lady Lovilocke were discreet. The two men shared a love of many of the same things: Scotch, Joyce, badminton and a certain serenity that they took to be the *sine qua non* of femininity.

But while Lord Lovilocke was never the jealous type, Hughes was. On occasion, Lady Lovilocke would have to remind Hughes that Lord Lovilocke was, after all, her husband. 'Only in law,' Harauld would reply, thus creating a new legal category. Harauld, as he would often remind her, could not respect the law for as long as the pubs shut so early. Like her, he was a romantic, and he had no intention of sharing her. The truth is, the two of them had fallen desperately, fatally in love . . .

Over the years, when discussing Hughes and Lady Lovilocke, people have paid a good deal of attention to the differences in their backgrounds. She the daughter of an aristocrat, and Hughes a man of mixed ancestry, with his wild hair, 'born in Wales no less'. But Lady Lovilocke and Hughes's joint life, for all its passion, was the life of the mind, and the mind knows no country, no class, no gender. It is a universal plain on which all are free to roam. But it is the artist who roams furthest and freest. As Lady Lovilocke puts it:

```
Harauld was such an artist, and part
of his artistry was helping me to be
an artist too or, in his more generous
words, to realise that I already was
one.
```

Their love was not about the securing of property or the joining of notable families, but about the mutually worshipful regard of two individuals whose exceptionalism had found its unique and counterbalancing equal.

For a short while, despite their boldness in eating at London's best restaurants and attending first nights together, Hughes and Lady Lovilocke managed to keep their affair a secret from their spouses. But it could not last.

```
November 23rd, 1976
Disaster! Ruination!
  Inevitably, perhaps, Felicity has found
out about Harauld and I and our love.
And though she may be the last person in
London to know, she's the first person
who seems intent on telling the rest of
the world. Even though she knows nothing,
she has told 'all' to the papers. I was
aware she was from the North but was ill-
prepared for her earthiness. The words
she has used about me are particularly
piquant — Harauld says he'll never
forgive her. She called me, among other
things, a 'home-wrecker'.
  'But YOU are my home!' Harauld said,
in a voice so loud that I woke in the
night with tinnitus. 'Why would you wreck
yourself?'
```

In November 1976, he was in the middle of writing *O Bedlam! O Bedlam!*, a film due to star . . . Felicity Stoat. Lovilocke and Hughes's affair risked a wreaking that went beyond the domestic.

4

UP THE ELEPHANT

LESLIE
Okay, let's try again.

THE ACTOR
I still don't understand who I'm
speaking to.

LESLIE
You're speaking to us, darling. The
whole piece is for us.

From *Prompt* (1965) by Harauld Hughes,
published by Faber & Faber

Dan has his top off. He says he's 'baking', but I think he just
wants to take his top off. Lying across the back seat of the van,
he talks about his artistic boundaries.

— I draw the line at filming paper. It's not cinematic.

The word 'cinematic' is most often used by people who work
in television. Of course, most films *are* 'filming paper', the paper
being the screenplay. I press the point.

— Isn't it interesting that the first thing Hughes wrote was a
play, and the last thing he wrote was a screenplay? It's what
Mick Barrett said: 'Film did for Harauld,' or something like
that.

Dan is playing a game on his phone.

– Why is that interesting?

– The way films destroy writers: Hemingway, Dorothy Parker, Faulkner, Fitzgerald . . .

– They take the money, though . . .

I imagine Dan at my deathbed, telling me to enjoy what's left of my life and not to focus on past mistakes.

– Don't you think it's also interesting that Hughes never wanted the script of *O Bedlam! O Bedlam!* to be published?

– Don't blame him. Who reads screenplays?

– I read screenplays!

– Yeah. But you're weird. In a good way. If you know what I mean.

– You mean there are two ways of being weird – a bad way and a good way – and I'm the good way?

– Is that a joke?

– I wouldn't close a set with it.

– I can't tell with you.

– Hughes published all his other screenplays. Why not this one?

– The film wasn't finished.

– But the *screenplay* was . . .

– Who would read a screenplay, let alone a screenplay of an unfinished film?

– I would!

– But you're weird, remember? The screenplay is like a souvenir of watching the film. It's not for reading.

– They should put that on the cover of more books: 'Not for reading purposes.'

– You know what I mean.

– That's the tragedy.

Dan weighs it. The question is whether to go to the Elephant and Castle library (it's literally across the street from us), where the Harauld Hughes collection is held. Perhaps they have a copy of *O Bedlam! O Bedlam!*

– All right, library boy, we can go, but let's not hang about. I reckon we rock up, get you bowling in – bit of chat with the bloke who runs the gaff – 'What's all the fuss about Harauld Hughes? – Is he legit? – Do you have any of his old screenplays? – Nice one – Do you mind if we take a cheeky look?' – have a thumb through – few reacts – up you get – cover you out – crack on with the next item.

I grew up in Elephant and Castle, and regardless of any subsequent redevelopments, it still consists primarily of a highly hostile, non-intuitive roundabout. Dan 'pans off it for a bit of interest', until the camera catches me walking along a busy street. I was not allowed to go out on these streets when I was a child. I was told the trees lining them were so diseased that they were, in effect, a chemical weapon.

Dan needs to take the shot again. There was something wrong with my microphone pack. I wonder what Tony Camera makes of it all. He's as silent as a BA co-pilot. Wiggsy Sound bounds over to adjust the settings.

– Bit lively round here.

He seems stoned already, or maybe everything *is* hilarious. On weekends, he services jacuzzis. He lives in Essex and says he's got enough work to last a lifetime.

– Footballers, mate.

His tone is confidential.

– I've seen things floating in jacuzzis you wouldn't believe.

I ask who his dealer is, and he touches the side of his nose.

– Government issue, mate.

———————

As I sit in the Elephant and Castle library, reading through its archive of Hughes's screenplays – complete with expanded drafts and excised scenes – I find myself electrified anew. There is an urgency to the writing, perhaps even greater than in his work for the theatre. The themes are familiar from the plays – violence, the feeling of being trapped, the thin line between illusion and reality – but here they have an intensity of action that is entirely its own. However, I am unable to find a copy of *O Bedlam! O Bedlam!*, and I can see how what I'm doing isn't terribly – to speak to Dan's concern – cinematic.

The librarian tells us that the only known complete screenplay of *Bedlam* is in a Swiss bank vault, along with all the footage from the film.

– You've heard of the legal case, I take it?

I turn to Dan. Maybe a flight to Geneva could be cinematic?

———————

We are at the bottom of Brook Drive, deep in Hughes country. I'm carrying a tripod, even though it's not my job to carry a tripod, because I'm the kind of person who will carry a tripod without thought of reward. Dan is concerned.

– I don't know if I can wangle Geneva, mate. This is all becoming a bit Dan Brown. A bit mystery-mystery. Don't know. It's a ball-ache to get crew. They don't do favours out there – everyone's on full whack. Plus, why is there only 'one known copy' of the script? Didn't they have photo-copiers in the 1970s? I mean, whether they finished the film or not, they *started* it, so every single department would have had a script. Art department, camera department, make-up department, costume . . .
– I know the departments . . .
– So why is there only 'one known copy'? How does that dusty geezer know? He's talking about it like it's the Rosanna Stone.
– Rosetta Stone.

Wiggsy's eyes clamp shut with laughter. His beard is dusted white from his pre-lunch doughnut. Dan is undeterred.

– I think what we *actually* need is some of Harauld's voice.

I hate the way he calls him Harauld. He doesn't know Harauld.

– Let's get a sequence of you going to the National Film Archive. Watching some old interviews. We know you like libraries.

Dan says 'libraries' like it's a kink.

– Why don't you just cut directly to Hughes being interviewed?
– I like keeping the sense of a journey.

Dan's way of keeping a sense of a journey is to show a journey, bookended by someone saying they are about to go on a journey and/or have just been on a journey, all the while staring at a moving landscape through a reflective surface, underpinned by a voice-over about being on a journey. His commitment to literalism is almost inspiring.

On the other hand, the national archive is just down the road. Tony Camera is on the phone to them now.

5

HUGHES ON FILM

                    IAN
I'm not interested in perfection. I'm
interested in what's real.

                    SOLVEIG
Am I real, Ian? Because I feel like I'm
in a dream.

                    IAN
Sometimes there's nothing more real
than a dream.

                    SOLVEIG
But what about reality?

                    IAN
What about it?

                    SOLVEIG
Isn't reality more real than a dream?

                    IAN
I suppose so. But who needs reality
when you can have the dream?

                    SOLVEIG
What if all you dream of is reality?

                    IAN
Then you don't have much of a dream.

From *The Swinging Models* (1966),
scr. Harauld Hughes, dir. Ibssen Anderssen,
published by Faber & Faber

A man from the National Film Archive called Simon leads me to
a little booth. The dominant colour is orange; the Archi(v)tèque
(the 'v' is silent) almost satirically evokes what people in the

1960s thought public spaces would resemble in the year 2000. I feel like Jacques Tati in my too-tight mac, bought before a bout of popcorn addiction that has compelled me to wear trousers with an elasticated waist. I ask the archivist how many hours of Harauld Hughes interviews they have at the Archi(v)tèque.

– More than you could watch in a day.
– So more than twenty-four hours?
– Oh, no. Less than that. Maybe seven hours.

I do a mental maths blink, and Simon walks out of shot. He turns to Dan and asks whether he should have expressed that differently, but Dan says that he shouldn't worry because it was funny, but if he ever *is* filmed again, he shouldn't speak until the director says 'cut', the director being him (Dan).

The archive curates a project called 'InVisIon', whose aim is to create a searchable database of interviews with 'prominent theatre and film practitioners: the iconoclasts and visionaries who have changed the landscape of our collected imagination'. Mavericks, grouped by type. The file we're here to see is called 'Harauld Hughes on Film' and was made to coincide with the premiere of *The Model and the Rocker*. It consists of a 16mm black-and-white close shot of Hughes's face, shot on location, intercut with the author walking moodily by the Thames, collar up, cigarette in hand, a gaze that says, 'So many stories, and only I can see them.' He wears a black polo neck and Philip Larkin glasses. He is covered in either sweat or drizzle. The brief voice-over, delivered by Hughes, runs thus:

```
They call film a director's medium.
But where is the director without
a script? I'm interested in that
```

68

```
dependency. The dependence the master
has on the slave. Perhaps it is not
merely his cruelty that leads the
master to despise himself, but also
his weakness for relying on his
servant.
    I am excited about entering this new
medium. I feel my work as a playwright
will only enrich the form, and my
experiences with film will bring new
dimensions to my work as a dramatist.
```

I ask Simon if he has anything of Hughes discussing
O Bedlam! O Bedlam!

– Well, for that you really want to hear what Leslie Francis has
  to say. I mean, he directed it, and given that Felicity Stoat's
  dead, he's the key witness.
– Do you have an interview with him?
– Not about *Bedlam*, no.
– Is he still with us?
– As in alive?
– Yes.
– No.

It's like telling someone they look like they could do with a
drink and then saying the bar is closed.

– There *is* quite an interesting clip of him reading from his
  film diaries. It's from a pilot of a show called *Dear Diary*.
  Semi-famous and/or relatively illustrious figures would
  read a passage from their diary, a little like *Jackanory*. But it
  didn't go past pilot stage.
– Why's that?

– I think the consensus was that it was a bit boring. Anyway, you're welcome to take a look.

– Dan?

– Well, says Dan, now that you've given it such a build-up, how can we resist?

I've learned that Dan will never avoid an utterance on the grounds of its obviousness.

Roll tape.

Leslie Francis is wearing a striped shirt, open at the neck; a lilac jumper jauntily hugs his shoulders. But for his professorial voice and half-moon glasses, secured by a canary cord, he could be an amateur yachtsman. His metre is commanding and clear, with a self-consciously theatrical sense of rhythm.

```
Hello. My name is Leslie Francis. I'm
a director of both film and theatre,
though I have worked in the theatre
more than film, and I also write about
film. What I am about to read to you is
one of the pieces I have written about
film, a film I had undertaken to direct
entitled O Bedlam! O Bedlam! I will
start to read it now.
```

Then a black screen with a caption – 'The following interview has been withdrawn for legal reasons and is no longer available' – scored by the sine-wave tone you used to hear on television late at night, under the test card.

Dan makes a face. Simon says he'll try to find out what's happened, but he won't find out what's happened, nor does he seem to have the capacity to find out.

Later that night, Charlie, our researcher in the office, solves the mystery. The interview was removed from the archive at the request of Lady Virginia Lovilocke.

We're interviewing her tomorrow. Should I mention this?

————————

Although we do not have the script for *O Bedlam! O Bedlam!*, we do have, oddly, an introduction to it. It was written by Hughes's biographer, Augustus Pink, for an edition of the screenplay which, days before publication, was withdrawn. Simon has given us a photocopy of a rare edition of the short-lived *Film Focus*, which repurposes the introduction as an article. He says photocopying the magazine without wearing gloves can damage it, and his special gloves are at the cleaner's, so we mustn't tell anyone what he's done. Wiggsy says that what Simon's done with his special gloves is between him and God. What follows first appeared in 1983:

> The shooting script differs from the continuity script. The former is what the director refers to before and during the production. As such, it is subject to change. The latter, by contrast, is a transcript of the finished film, and largely exists as a way of copyrighting the picture as a 'text'; with its bloodless logging and description, it is scarcely more evocative than a legal document.
>
> The shooting script is more poetic, conveying mood, even motivation, though this mood and its motivation may be discarded on the harsh terrain of the film set. Ordinarily, those not involved with the making of the film would read such a script only after watching the film. It feels indecorous to read a published screenplay in advance of watching it, like a fiancé visiting his young bride-to-be the night before her wedding. Can he not wait to see her in her full glory? Only after the film

has been properly projected and digested – and ideally on more than one occasion – might one dare to read a printed copy of the scenario, and always with the completed film in mind. As such, one's mind's eye gives the characters the faces of the relevant actors, and when the dialogue is read, it is heard with the recalled intonation of the selected take.

O Bedlam! O Bedlam! is different. We have the screenplay, but not the film. We know whom Leslie Francis cast, but we haven't seen how his cast interpreted the roles. We hear the dialogue but have no memory of its inflection. The film was shot (mostly) and edited (partially) but never released, and if we believe the rumours, resides in a Swiss vault, unlikely ever to emerge.

However, the film, by which I mean the shooting script, reads remarkably well. It is a work that would have been very pertinent in the mid-1970s but is perhaps even more pertinent now. A satire? Certainly. A lament? Very much so. An elegy? Yes, I think it is. A eulogy? Perhaps. That would have depended on the tone. And that tone remains a mystery. For very few have seen what remains of the film, and even fewer have seen what some claim is a four-hour work print. One of them was *O Bedlam! O Bedlam!*'s director, Leslie Francis. One might only wonder how Francis might have interpreted and, indeed, altered the story both on set and in the cutting room, had he ever made it *into* the cutting room. But perhaps one should not expect him to have strayed too far from Hughes's original conception. Mickie Perch, the producer of *Bedlam* and many other Hughes scripts, told me:

Leslie needs writers, and he hates that. He wishes he could write, and he certainly is a very good critical writer – of articles, monographs and so forth. He can bang out a hell of a foreword and a pretty decent afterword – it's the stuff in between that eludes him. The 'words', I suppose you'd call them. You see, Leslie – and he would be the first to admit this, if sufficiently pressed – lacks the ability to invent. He made a couple of tentative stabs at the fictive, but it never really came off. When Leslie wrote fiction himself, he knew it wasn't true, if that makes sense. And if Leslie didn't believe it was true, he had no access to his directorial gifts, which were utterly based on truth. His question was always, 'Is this what would *really* happen?' So imagine that sensibility colliding with a script about killer prawns [e.g. in the denouement of *The Model and the Rocker* (1968)]. He would ask, 'But how long can they survive out of water? Why do they want to kill? And how come they can also fly?'

But the Leslie Francis who came to direct *O Bedlam! O Bedlam!* did rather regard himself as a writer. His iconoclastic film *And . . .?!* had been feted on the Continent, not least for its innovative punctuation, but also for its screenplay, which Francis co-authored. He had started out in documentary and wrote the famous introduction to his 'discovered poem' *As Far West as Wales*:

> Mushrooms packed,
> Mushrooms stacked
> High in trucks
> And off to town.
>
> Wrenched from sod
> By wind-chapped hands.
> Cups gone soft
> In God's dank soil.
>
> A mug of tea,
> Then a smoke or two
> For Sidney sat
> Behind the wheel.

73

All this night
And through dawn too,
On to Nottingham
And beyond.

(Extract from *As Far West as*
Wales, dir. Leslie Francis)

But Francis was looking to move into a different type of
space, as he said in this interview from 1968:

Now, what we do in documentary is we record, and
then we shape. In other words, there is the process of
filming, or 'capturing' the subject, but then there is an
equally important stage, that of editing, or 'constructing'
a narrative. Because, in making a documentary, one is not
following a story – or certainly not a pre-planned story –
and here is where one requires patience – *one waits for story*
to emerge. One might say that if you follow anything for
long enough, a story will emerge, because 'story' is how
we make sense of the past, which is why it's so dangerous
to apply it to the future, why it's fatal to speculate. It's a
projection. So, one might say that story is a way of keeping
time in order.

To a man like Mickie Perch, who said he couldn't truly
love any film unless it featured nunchucks, the word 'patience'
was a red flag. Perch regarded time as an enemy, attacking
his profits and the temperaments of his girlfriends, many of
whom, grown cynical with age, would leave him and return to
college.

Rehearsing theatre was cheap. Rehearsing on set, while
the cast and crew racked up enormous hotel bills, was not.
Francis's process was slow and additive, it required revision,
improvisation, privacy. And time . . . Long stretches of it.

74

Francis spoke to me once about the difference between the theatre and the cinema, in terms of being an artist:

Theatre is like having the subject in front of you, for as long as you want (to all intents and purposes), as you build up a portrait in layers – as if using a soft crayon. Then, one day, the character is there. They are in the room with you. So much of the impact of theatre comes from being in the presence of the actors, a presence that is created over time. The economics – and the closest we come to an ethical scheme in this country is economics – reflects this. In a cinema all the seats cost the same, more or less – sometimes it's a few quid more for some extra leg room – but one expects a comparable experience throughout the auditorium. Different story in theatre. It can sometimes cost ten times as much to sit near the front as compared to the cheap seats in the balcony. *And that's because it's worth it.* The experience is entirely changed by proximity. The tension alters. I feel this is because time cannot be manipulated in the theatre. Of course, there is ellipsis, but each scene plays out in real time. In motion pictures, yes, much of the tension is created by the director's choice of where the camera is positioned in relation to the action – which, of course, means the lens (wide or long, deep focus or shallow), light, decor, costume, hair, before one even gets to the actors themselves or the words – but the true measure of cinematic presence is time. How long should we look at *this* rather than *that*? For how long am I present to *that* rather than *this*? Now that is not something a writer can control. A writer can only suggest. It is the director who brings the audience into the story. The director is the film.

Harauld Hughes seems to corroborate this:

During filming, though I am on the set, I prefer to look away. It's like watching someone else give birth every day, seven days a week for six weeks, and you have no idea when or how the baby will be born, or if you'll like it when the hell's over. No husband should attend the birth of his child. It's too painful.

Mostly, during Hughes's terrible ordeals, the person 'labouring' was Ibssen Anderssen. And Anderssen had, to continue the metaphor, sturdy hips. Although Leslie Francis received a co-directing credit on *The Glowing Wrong*, he shot only one day's extra footage; his primary contribution was supervising the edit after Anderssen went to an Oslo rehab facility to kick an antihistamine addiction. *O Bedlam! O Bedlam!* represented Francis's sole filmic collaboration with Hughes. But Francis couldn't 'deliver'. Why?

Francis addressed some of the rumours, albeit obliquely, in his film diaries, *Try Telling the Truth, Leslie!* Its publication entrenched the rift between him and Hughes. I will not revisit its outrageous accusations in this introduction, as Hughes has been gracious enough to confess to many of his own wrongdoings:

Yes, I did throw Leslie out of a helicopter. My only regret is that the helicopter was still on the ground. Virginia and I had chartered it so that I could get the hell away from that set. Mickie came running up and tried to get on board, just as the rotor blades were starting up. Felicity, my then-wife, was behind him, screaming, 'No, Mickie! Nooo!' I was kicking out, and Mickie bit into the heel of my foot. Leslie, who I hoped would see things from my perspective, tried to calm me down, so I suggested, physically, that he leave the helicopter. He accepted my suggestion and tumbled into Mickie and Felicity. Finally, the pilot just skied it. I turned to Virginia and said, 'Welcome to show business.'

Musing on the film's collapse, Leslie was quoted as saying, 'I'm a symbolist and a humanist; Harauld is a surrealist and a bastard.' To which Harauld replied, 'Leslie may be a humanist, but he's barely human; his only symbol is himself . . . Something happens to certain people when they direct a film: it acts as a growth hormone for self-regard. Leslie became a tyrant, a sadist and, worse, a bore.'

The final rupture, though, came on the literary plain, when Hughes wrote to Francis, a few years after *Bedlam*, about starting a new play. Hughes hadn't written one since 1972's *Dependence*, which Francis had directed, so it must have taken some courage for him to approach Francis with an idea for a piece entitled *Lines*:

It will consist, entirely, of lines that have been excised from my previous works. I have them in a file. And yes, Leslie, I do reread my work for pleasure. I'm able to be honest enough about the fact that I like my own writing very much. Indeed, I'm one of my favourite writers. And I've made a point of instructing my secretary to keep every line that has been cut from one of my plays or screenplays or poems. She types them out on a single sheet of A4 paper and then safeguards them in a file – well, several files actually. Looking through them has often sparked a new work – a piece for the theatre or a scenario for the cinema. I thought it could be interesting to develop this decontextualising dislocation – a type of non-linearity – for a longer piece. Because for me – and now for the actors – each line is like a Rosetta Stone, an aide-memoire for a longer piece of text, so the completed poems, plays and scripts from which these lines were cut would become the discarded material of *this* piece.

Best, Harauld.

Francis's reply, scrawled on a postcard:

> So am I right in thinking that both types of work could be
> regarded as waste material?

> Is it callous to consider the loss of *O Bedlam! O Bedlam!*
> greater than that of their friendship? Relationships often
> become infected and die, but their film would have lived on
> for ever. We weep for it.

> *Augustus Pink is a critic and biographer specialising in post-war*
> *British theatre.*

I feel like I'm trying to lasso smoke. I want to know why
O Bedlam! O Bedlam! foundered. Hearing how good it might
have been is tantalising, but of little use.

I'm outside the Archi(v)tèque. Dan has asked Tony Camera
to grab something from the shoulder; there's no time to set up
the tripod – we're losing the light. I look out towards the river.
I consider what has been lost, the images we will never see. I see
someone body-popping.

— But a man dying of thirst might not be able to choose his
   ideal refreshment. He must drink what he is given.

Wiggsy smirks.

The word I would use in an English essay to describe this kind
of light, to get marks for ambitious vocabulary, is 'vermilion'.

— Simon [my tone is laden with mystery] has given us one
   more piece of source material.

There isn't even time to set up the autocue. I'm making this up.

– And I'm holding it in my hand.

I hold up a brown envelope long enough for Tony Camera to zoom in for a closer shot.

– It's a letter from Leslie Francis dated February 8th, 1977, when *Bedlam* was in pre-production.

I open the envelope. I let the camera record the moment of discovery, before fixing the lens with a look that says, 'And on we go.'

– This is what Leslie says.

My dear Felicity [Stoat],
I don't think we need repeat much of what we discussed so late into the night, not just because certain accusations shouldn't be set down in print, but also because you sounded drunker than you were willing to admit. I shudder at the very thought of the hotel bill; I hope I can rely on you to cover the cost out of your own pocket – the film budget cannot absorb such profligacy. However, as it's almost dawn and I haven't a chance of going back to sleep, I thought it might be worth setting out – briefly – a few matters so that we might move forward.
  1. I believe that Harauld has acted appallingly. His actions have betrayed not only your marriage – not that I think marriage has any particular value – but also your talent – a much greater sin – not that I believe in sin. The least he could have done was to wait until the film was over and done with before he told you about Virginia. Well, told you he has – so you will have to put it out of your mind for the next few

79

months at least. We have a film to make, and make it we will. Not all the scenes will call for tears.

2. The character you are playing requires a deftness and lightness of touch. Grief, no matter how justified on a personal level, will prove an impenetrable barrier to a worthwhile portrayal. It's simply a choice. Wallow in this muck or wade out of it.

3. We talked much about the veracity of *his* protestations but, I have to put it to you, did *you* ever really love Harauld? When you met, you were a star (and you still are, though you seem to have forgotten this) – which is to say, he was not yet 'Harauld Hughes'. He was an actor with an overly loud voice who unwisely thought himself a poet. And while his speaking voice has become no more nuanced, he has found – we must admit – a writing voice. And we have all benefited from this voice in various ways. You are Harauld Hughes's wife (for the moment at least). Whenever you act in one of his creations – be it on stage or on screen – you are playing two parts: the character and the part of Harauld Hughes's wife being cast in a Harauld Hughes production. You worry that you are seen as 'an obligatory presence'. Any sense of merit you once had for being cast has vanished. You've been *swallowed* like Jonah, you say. But let us not forget that the whale *saves* Jonah. Without the whale, he would have drowned. You say Harauld's 'genius has destroyed any sense I might have of being a person'. I would say that anyone who is lessened by genius is not much of a person, for genius is in short supply. Having said that, I consider Harauld an unreliable supplier. He reminds one of the elusive good oyster. They're rarely on the menu, and when they are, they're often off.

4. Harauld is like a scared little boy – and like all scared little boys, he's gone running for his mother. Enter Virginia. Figuratively. Literally. Could a name be any less etymologically apposite?

5. You are not Harauld's mother. As such, you have not acted as if you were his mother. This may have been your fatal error.

80

It has led to the erroneous assumption that you can have an equal relationship with him. But we know Harauld must either dominate or be dominated. I am happy to be dominated. You, less so. Harauld has become Virginia's worshipful disciple. An acolyte. But of what? His own return to infancy.

6. Yes – Harauld has given you many parts over the years. You took these parts. Was this an error? The question is unimportant. You took them. I don't think you should regard the *work* you did as substandard per se – it was always perfectly fine, even though (in my view) you were miscast as the vamp. Yours is a homely beauty. And, yes, that home is now empty, and perhaps it will be repossessed. But . . .

7. This means that, finally, in your forties (and looking it) you have the opportunity to become a person, and not a self-important writer's idea of one. I would grasp this chance; it may be your last. Personally, and the pun is unintentional, I would love to become a human being, though I fear I'm too lost in this dreadful persona of mine.

Over to you.
As ever, in admiration and hope,
Leslie

– So, outside of *Herstory*, the extant written materials pertaining to *Bedlam* consist of an epistolary pep talk and a published introduction to an unpublished script. Not too much to go on. What happened on set? And who took off in that heli-copter? I need to speak to the woman who knew Harauld better than anyone else. I need to speak to Lady Virginia Lovilocke. And that . . . is what I'm going to do now.

I saunter past the lens. Tony Camera's happy. Thumbs up from Dan.

That's the one.

6

A FRAME WITHOUT A PICTURE

He has poured his meagre essence into
his work. I cannot respect any man who
works. Work repels me — its incessant
need for timetabling, its triviality,
its counterfeit promise of redemption.

From *Roost* (1962) by Harauld Hughes,
published by Faber & Faber

I am staring at morphing slices of light on the wall, made globular by midnight rain, when the banging starts. The noise is
coming from the room next door. I feel a rush of fear. If I were a
squid, I'd have dropped the ink by now. What order of derange-
ment would lead someone to bang on the walls of a Novotel?
(The Travel Tavern was full.) The walls in such 'hotels' are not
merely thin; they're sonic amplifiers. Everyone here is exhausted.
If we were any less exhausted, we would be using our remaining
energy to leave the Novotel. We are, essentially, cellmates, the
co-inhabitants of what is, to all intents and purposes, a giant
snare drum.

I will not be able to sleep. I will not be able to think. I will
not be able to form a coherent line of enquiry, and without a
coherent line of enquiry, what is one left with? A perhaps too literal interpretation of the word 'interview': a sad stretch of silent
staring. There's an argument to be made that staring is not much
better than banging. Banging, you could argue, at least displays
a communicative impulse.

I uncrumple tomorrow's questions:

'Lady Virginia, it is the twentieth anniversary of Harauld Hughes's death. What do you imagine he would think of the theatre now?'

'What made Harauld Hughes such a unique writer?'

'How do you feel he'll be remembered in twenty more years?'

'How do *you* hope he'll be remembered?'

'Do you have a favourite work of his?'

But what I really want to ask Lady Lovilocke is, 'Why did Harauld Hughes stop writing?' The reason I won't ask that question is because Received Opinion has already answered it. The Received Opinion is: Harauld Hughes stopped writing because he married Lady Virginia Lovilocke. Was this down to guilt for the callous way Hughes ended his relationship with his first wife, Felicity Stoat? Was Stoat the not-so-secret inspiration behind his work? Was it the creative entropy that often descends on artists, especially those whose initial energy springs from anger, as the thicket of middle age begins to obscure the horizon? How angry can you be when you become successful, rich, in love? Did Hughes stop writing because he was . . . happy? Or perhaps he simply got stuck, as Lady Virginia Lovilocke suggests:

> Once, after we made love, Harauld seemed troubled. I asked him why, and whether I'd done something wrong. With his unerring gallantry he said I was incapable of doing anything wrong, that it simply wasn't in my nature. He was in the middle of writing a film, he told me, and it was absolute hell. 'Then why don't you stop writing it?' I asked, already knowing that the answer, if there were to be an answer (for Harauld had already revealed himself to be disinclined to answer anything without giving due attention to the question's complexity), would be far from simple. Just how far from simple became the story of the next year or so, and involved the break-up

of two marriages, a mini-stroke, an unproved homicide and a media circus that led to a period of crippling writer's block for Harauld that was to last – in many ways – until his death. The film, of course, was *O Bedlam! O Bedlam!* An apt title, it turned out.

Biographers might note that one of the first questions Lady Lovilocke asked Hughes was, 'Why don't you stop writing . . .?'

I have watched several clips of Lady Lovilocke's television appearances, and though she charms with the bemused smile that often accompanies hereditary wealth, she also possesses an incapacity to hide her disdain for those not quite up to the mark. I don't want her to point out my inadequacies, nor compare me (unfavourably) to Hughes. You see, Hughes means a good deal to me, and I am frightened of meeting someone who meant a good deal to Hughes and, further, viewed him as *l'homme idéal.* For the mute gaze of an ill-read catatonic is pretty far from *idéal.* I fear I may get the full force of her derision. And if I do manage to prise open my mouth, what will she hear? The nasal bleat of a dead-eyed introvert. It's hell. Hopeless. All is death.

At which point the banging stops.

I'm still awake two hours later, when I hear my phone ping.

– Her ladyship's sacked us off. Stand by. D Dog.

Lady Lovilocke has cancelled. An 'unexpected family matter'. At her age (eighty-eight), what family matter, excepting resurrection, *could* be unexpected?

7

OUT OF THE PINK
(AND INTO THE BLACK)

<pre>
              SHE
You do anything. To protect those you
love.

              HE
Yes. And the unloved?

              SHE
The unloved?

              HE
Should we protect them?
</pre>

From *Flight* (1964) by Harauld Hughes,
published by Faber & Faber

Dan is talking.

— I think we got some great stuff yesterday. The stuff with
Mick Barrett, and even moments in the library. It's going to
boil down a treat.

I try to picture this. The pain of so doing must be registering
on my face.

— Obviously not all of it. Simon was pretty boring. But that's
why there's an edit.

He leans forward, his lips speckled from a second macchiato.

– And is all good from your point of view? Probably too early to tell, right?

I don't answer quickly enough. Here is a man for whom a forced compliment will do just as well.

– I mean, are you enjoying it? he continues.

I do not know this from experience, but if your profession is considered worthwhile, the question of one's enjoyment is seldom invoked.
'What do you do?'
'I am an orthopaedic surgeon.'
'And do you enjoy it?'
I can't shake the suspicion that the only explanation people can accommodate is that doing something as pointless as 'presenting' must engender an almost overwhelming rush of pleasure; that a life of triviality and inconsequence is the price I must pay for such unimaginable joy. I close my copy of *Herstory*.

– I'm not terrific at enjoying things.

It's hard to know if this is merely shtick or whether it has become true through years of compartmentalisation.

– But that's no reflection on everyone else, I add.

I sense I'm still some way off the genuine approbation the D-Meister seems to require, so I offer a concession.

– I'm very grateful.

Perhaps his laugh is genuine. Dan then explains that today's (hastily arranged) interview with Augustus Pink is to be the 'spine' of the documentary.

– Once we've done this, we've broken the back of the doc.

There's something barbaric about Dan's contractions.
Tony Camera is driving the van today. We need to save money to make up for moving the schedule around.

———————

Hughes, on receiving the 1986 Euripides Prize for short-form drama, said something that pertained to his work for the stage, but perhaps it applies equally to his work for the screen:

> I have always wanted my plays to speak for themselves, not
> I for them. Further, for me, to write a play *is* to speak. In
> the periods when I am unable to write because I am making
> love, or am too angry to make love, a sadness descends.
> A sadness to do with this highly temporary inability to
> communicate to my fellow man. Perhaps I could solve this by
> making love to my fellow man, but I hope I can say, without
> inflection, that I am simply incapable of this most ancient
> Greek of acts. I checked.

So might we consider him an unhappy man for the last thirty years of his life? For the span of his second marriage to Lady Lovilocke?
And yet.

In her introduction to *The Collected Shorter Works of Harauld Hughes* (published by Faber & Faber), Lady Lovilocke describes the two of them being 'despite fortune's vagaries . . . in a bubble of bliss'. And, furthermore, she speaks of a Harauld who is still writing or, as Zweig might put it, 'struggling with the Daemon'. This, from *Herstory*:

> Often, in the middle of the night . . . a story would erupt within him, and I would feel a sudden rush of air as the bedsheets flew off. Harauld would leap out of bed and stride around the ottoman, demanding pen and paper, and once I'd located them, he would write with stabbing fury until the words had left him. It was a possession, a visitation, during which he would be overtaken by images and torrents of words. His role, he felt, was simply to listen, and to help the words and images find their right order.

She adds:

> When Harauld began to work, he would have no idea as to the length of the play that he was writing. But after a day or two, he might get a sense. 'This one's a short one,' he would say, or, 'I have a feeling this one might be long. Or longish.' Often, something he initially thought might turn out long would end up being short, or vice versa. These moments were especially exciting; the air around him would positively thrum with electricity. 'I thought it would be short, but it's actually quite long!' he would say, shooing a child back into the loving arms of a housekeeper.

But if this is true, where *is* the work? Where *are* these words that burst from him with such fury?

In one of his introductions to *The Harauld Hughes Half-Hour*

Plays, Hughes discusses the matter of playwrighting with God (played by Edmund Butterby):

```
                    GOD
    . . . how long can it take to write a
play?

                  HARAULD
Perhaps it is more difficult to write a
play than it is to make the world.

                    GOD
Perhaps.

Silence.

                    GOD
But roughly . . . how long? For a play?

                  HARAULD
A play should come out in one go. Like
a tooth.
```

I suppose what I'm saying is, we're missing some teeth. Maybe more than a mouthful. And I'm hoping that Augustus Pink will be able to locate some of these errant choppers.

———

When one sees the name Augustus Pink, the imagination strains at the moniker. How could someone live up to it? But upon meeting him, it is soon apparent that no other nomenclature will do. Under Pink's linen jacket (a crumpled oatmeal) he wears, of course, a soft pink shirt that is fraying slightly at the cuffs. His trousers manage to be both tasteful and (there's no use denying it) mustard, while his boat shoes (he's just been doing a spot of weeding) have the well-worn look of a lifetime's gentle use. He seems somewhat bemused when I decline his offer of a glass of Chardonnay. 'Why would you turn down wine?' seems to be the gist. 'It's almost time for lunch.' In fact, Wiggsy nobly takes up the slack and downs the best part of a bottle. Unsteady and acidic, he affixes a wind cover to my radio mic to ward off the south-westerlies wafting across the well-tended lawn of Pink's South Richmond abode.

– Hopefully we won't get hammered by Heathrow.
– I don't think we can blame Heathrow for your being hammered, I say.

Pink, gallant, intercedes.

– That's probably my fault. But it's so lovely in the garden.
– Don't make much difference, Wiggsy offers. Inside, outside – we still have to stop if there's a fly-past. Planes, mate. Bane of my life.
– Isn't that interesting . . .

Pink bows his head, briefly, as if weighing the burden of the professional sound recordist in a world filled with extraneous noise.

– . . . I suppose they must be.

Pink narrows his eyes. He seems to give words more syllables than they contain.

– So you're the pre-se-nt-er?
– I don't know what I am.
– Well, let's find out.

– I think the aim is for me to find out who you are.
– I have to say I still don't exactly know what all this is in aid of.
– Well, it's twenty years since Hughes died . . .

I drop my voice on the word 'died' so that he knows I regard death as a serious matter, but I end up making it sound like a venereal disease.

– So I suppose the documentary is to mark that and hopefully bring his work back to the public's attention.

Pink smiles the smile of someone accustomed to rebuffing rank and file.

– Is this what you do?
– How do you mean?
– I suppose I mean . . . television.

He says the word 'television' with the tentativeness one reserves for reporting the use of a racial slur to a Similarly Shocked Liberal.

– I'm more of a writer. Television helps afford me the time to write.
– I would have thought television would use up time that could be spent writing.

This is exactly what has happened.

– This might not be on television.

If I had a forelock, I'd be tugging it.

– It's an independent, self-financed production, so it could
  end up playing festivals first.
– Could it really? What a prospect.

A pause.

– Well, I wish you luck with your television programme. Not
  that Harauld believed in luck. Shall we begin?

Pink is the world expert on Harauld Hughes and, by self-
admission, an acolyte. In his postscript to Harauld Hughes's
Table (available in *The Collected Works of Harauld Hughes*), Pink
sets out his stall:

I make no apology for my admiration of Hughes. Mine is the
zeal of the convert. I resisted him at first, feeling his work to
be brittle, inhumane, unemotional. Perhaps because the first
play of his I saw was *Table*. I didn't get it. I was expecting
something gritty, northern even (*Platform* had already
permeated the air). What I saw seemed to be a comedy of
manners. Something suburban and shallow. I accused Hughes
of glibness in my two-star review 'Turning the *Table*', a charge
that I would live to both regret and, mercifully, recant. After
the article, which received the approbation of my peers,
Hughes sent me a telegram: 'Shall we have a drink.' No
question mark; assent was implied.
    We met at noon, at perhaps the Connaught. Hughes
ordered a bottle of vintage champagne. I informed him that
I couldn't afford, on a reviewer's salary, to pay for a glass, let

alone a bottle. 'They pay you?' he asked. He seemed sincere, but this is the modus of the piss-taker: you must syphon with dispassion. 'Anyway, this isn't "a drink"; champagne is something to keep you going until the drinking starts. And the Scotch here is perfectly affordable.' Not that he let me pay. We did, indeed, go on with whisky. But Hughes likes to finish what he started, so we went back to champagne.

Later, I woke up on a snooker table in Aldwych. Harauld was standing over me. He asked me what I thought a story was. I told him. When I had finished, he said, 'I've never heard so much shit in my life.' And he was right. What I had said was shit. But his saying that didn't make *me* feel shit. The shit was out of me now. It had been expelled from my mouth and, from the look of the felt, through my flannels. Hughes had me cleaned and dried before his driver dropped me home. I had a three-day hangover. I remember it being three days because the light still hurt my eyes when I opened the door to take delivery of a new suit that Hughes had sent me. The accompanying note said, 'And on the third day he rose again.' That night I stuck to beer. We talked about theatre, badminton, Yeats and the exhausting logistics of marital betrayal.

Two years later, I went to watch a revival of *Table* at the Royal Court and found myself watching an entirely new play. Or rather, I found the same play, but I was made new. In my review, 'Resetting the *Table*', I made about as sharp a 180 as I could manage. 'Hughes, it is clear, is our best playwright, not simply because of the quality of the words, but because of the quality of everything *between the words* . . . His is a theatre of omission in which verbal dexterity serves to obscure something darker, lurking (literally) beneath . . . The revival of *Table* is more than a triumph. It's an act of revisionism. But it's the audience that has to reform. The playwright's crime was one of prescience. A prescience that was perhaps too much for us. As T. S. Eliot said, man can bear only so much reality. Is there anything more real than Harauld Hughes?'

That night Hughes wrote me another telegram: 'Perhaps mankind can only bear so much Hughes. But if you can bear to have another drink with me, I'll buy the first few.'

Hughes and Pink became friends, united by their love of the arts and their mutual thirst for anything fermented. Throughout the years, when other critics were suggesting that Hughes's creative reservoir was running dry, Pink remained a vehement apologist, publishing the famous article 'Why Should Writers Write?', in which he claimed that Hughes's silence was more creatively generative than the combined sum of all the remaining writers in Europe.

———————

The camera is set up, and Dan, again too loud, calls 'Action!'

- Hughes wrote his last play in 1972. He wrote his last screen-play in 1976. Why are we still talking about him?
- I suppose because people like you are still asking about him. That would be the short answer.
- And what would the long answer be?
- Touché.

I look over at Dan, who seems to be thinking, 'But "touché" is even shorter.'

- Would you call Hughes a friend of yours?
- He was gracious enough, for a time, to call me one of his. And I was very grateful for that.

– What was Hughes like as a friend?
– Fiercely loyal. Tender. Exacting. Punctual.
– Did you ever fall out?
– Frequently.
– When did you last speak?
– We last spoke about ten years before he won the Euripides Prize.
– In 1986?
– The Euripides Prize was awarded to Harauld Hughes in 1986.
– So you last spoke to him in 1976?
– Around then, yes. More like '77. Spring or summer of '77. But we stayed in touch via letters for about three weeks after that.
– Why did you stop speaking?
– I didn't.

A Hughesian pause.

– Were you close to Felicity Stoat?
– I knew her. But by the time I met Harauld, they were living rather separate lives.
– Did Hughes ever speak about her?
– Hughes, as I mentioned, was very loyal.
– How did that sense of loyalty play into his affairs? And, I suppose, most significantly, his affair with Lady Virginia Lovilocke?
– Plane! shouts Wiggsy.

———

In 1976, Harauld Hughes and Lady Virginia Lovilocke left their respective spouses and took what they called a 'modest' suite (in fact, most of the top floor of the Dorchester), where they could shelter from the squall of press intrusion, with its localised tempests of invective and slurs. According to Lady Lovilocke, she and Hughes coped 'only with God's grace (a grace in which Harauld strongly disbelieved) and by cleaving close to one another'.

Hughes was protective by nature, and each morning, as Lady Lovilocke picked anxiously at her melon and prosciutto, she had a high-angle view from their balcony of 'darling Harauld' fighting the various photographers massed in front of the entrance lobby. Lovilocke's estranged husband bore the separation from Virginia with remarkable sangfroid, and he and Hughes became, if not intimate, then something close to collegiate. They even played badminton on one memorable occasion, but Hughes gave him such a fearsome thrashing (for Hughes hadn't the capacity to hold back on the court any more than in matters of the heart) that Lord Langley's personal physician made him swear a solemn oath that he would never play Hughes again. Meanwhile, Felicity Stoat, to complicate an already complex situation, was still contracted to be the star of *O Bedlam! O Bedlam!* (which Harauld was frantically rewriting), but this did little to staunch her outpouring of fury to the tabloids.

Much of *Herstory: My Time with Harauld Hughes* is Virginia Lovilocke's attempt to bring to light the events of this tempestuous time, an endeavour fraught with difficulty . . .

The title of this book serves as both promissory note and disclaimer. It is not the story of our lives. How could I tell it in one volume, and why would I want to reveal so much? It is, instead, the story of the only one of his screenplays that Harauld regarded as unfinished. The failure of *O Bedlam! O Bedlam!*, and Harauld's attendant disappointment, is inextricable from the story of the beginning of our life in common, which, though we remained together until Harauld's death some thirty years later (and a more blissful thirty years I cannot imagine), I also regard as unfinished. For though Harauld has left this mortal realm, I believe we will be reunited in heaven and that our love is without end. Conversely, this is also a story about the breakdown of our previous marriages, but perhaps one could view them, given our failings within them, as unfinished too. The entanglements that involve children can never come to an end, even should we so wish. And, perhaps lastly – and the import of the 'perhaps' may come into focus over the course of this book – it is a story about the unfinished nature of stories themselves. Harauld loathed the notion of the omniscient narrator. To him, all stories were unfinished, continuing to develop with each telling, each viewing. Harauld felt that even when a story was forgotten, it didn't die; it lay dormant, waiting to re-emerge.

It has been said that the enduring theme of Hughes's work is loss. So perhaps it is fitting that much of Lady Lovilocke's book should concern itself with a lost film. Film is a peculiar medium. On the one hand, it is an art form, and on the other, it is a confection to be consumed; a creation of no greater solemnity or substance than a meringue, and one that must be sold quickly, before it collapses, to make way for the next batch. Hughes was avowedly unable to write on demand, which might be why filmmaking, with its schedules, call sheets and release dates, ultimately proved so wearisome for him. But there was another reason Lovilocke thought it important to set pen to paper:

I suppose, at some unconscious level, I was aware I had embarked on a life with one of the most extraordinarily creative minds of the modern era, and I knew it was important to document it. Having said that, I have often wondered whether I should publish this book at all. Some have told me that I shouldn't, that there has been enough controversy, and that the greatest dignity lies in silence. But Harauld didn't believe in dignity. And I rather wonder whether it is at Harauld's urging that I am undertaking this necessarily unfinishable project, for it is his spirit, his sense of 'play', that infuses all that follows. As one would expect, Harauld loved to cause a scene, and to that extent I think he would love this book. He was always encouraging me to be less polite. I hope, with this modest offering, I've in some way managed to take his advice.

Although I think of myself as a theologian, I would not reject the title of biographer either, for in trying to understand the lives of the saints – and I believe Harauld was a secular saint – we must learn to understand and appreciate people.

So these are my confessions. May God, and Harauld, forgive me.

And may Pink forgive me.

In what feels like a slow-motion acknowledgement of the distant concerns of others, we wait for the faraway rush of air to recede. The thrumming whoosh one hears inside an aeroplane is called 'pink noise'.

I decide against mentioning this.

Wiggsy presses his headphones to the side of his head, slowly raises his index finger, then drops it like a baton.

– We were talking about Hughes's idea of loyalty and his affair
with Lady Virginia Lovilocke . . .
– We weren't talking about that at all. You asked a prurient
question, and then a passing plane robbed me of the opportunity to make my distaste immediately apparent.
– Our documentary is trying to ask why Hughes stopped
writing. And the fact is, this does coincide with his relationship with Lady Virginia Lovilocke. With leaving Felicity
Stoat. I'm surprised that you don't cover these events more
fully in your biography of Hughes.
– My biography of Hughes is a serious piece of literary
criticism, delving, often deeply, into one of our major playwrights. That's why it's called *Harauld Hughes: The Work*.
It is not a tabloid exposé. With respect to the relationship between Harauld and Virginia, and indeed between
Harauld and any of his lovers, I felt that had been covered –
and covered rather well, I thought – in Virginia's book.
– In *Herstory*?
– Yes.
– But your critical biography preceded *Herstory* – by twenty
years. How could you have known what Lady Lovilocke
was going to cover?
– I was referring to the revised edition of my book [*Harauld
Hughes: The Work* (revised and updated edition)], which
came out recently, after Virginia's book, and which is the
real reason I've agreed to talk to you.
– To promote that.
– I don't think any of us are here purely for our health. As
Renoir said, 'We each have our reasons.'
– Yes – 'The truly terrible thing is that everybody has their
reasons.'

— How clever of you to remember the full quote.

— So you are unable to talk about how Hughes's marriage breakdown may have affected him as a writer?

— I am unwilling, rather than unable.

— Because I wonder whether it *is* worth talking about.

— Well, I leave you to your wonderings.

———————

To say that Lady Virginia did not hold Felicity Stoat in high esteem is to put the matter mildly. Much of *Herstory* is devoted to passages of scarcely disguised savagery:

'Felicity' was a word for which I had a great feeling until I met Harauld's first and thankfully former wife. It means 'a state of great happiness'. And while Felicity certainly was in a state, it was not of happiness. It was a great state of self-pity, an unbending principality whose governing body was ossified in ire; she was the jealous keeper of an ever-expanding inventory of accumulated injustices visited upon her by (it seemed) everyone she had ever met, and quite a few whom she hadn't. In Felicity's unaltering thesis, her life's misfortunes began in earnest when she took up with Harauld: once a *tabula rasa*, now fatally scored by him. Opportunities shattered like a brittle skiff on the cliffs of his indifference, or so the charge went. Casting directors were blind to her versatility ever since she took on the mantle of the archetypical Hughesian woman: the cold, scrutinising manipulator of men. They say you write what you know, and perhaps Harauld hadn't had the opportunity to see the nurturing side of Woman until his middle years. He once confided to me, 'Before you, Virginia, all women were scolding mothers or hardened harlots. You have delivered me, shown me a love that I didn't know existed.' I told him I appreciated his comments very much. A tear glistened in his eye. I don't know that he had ever been spoken to so warmly.

Lady Lovilocke then proceeds, with chill appraisal, to dismantle Stoat's standing as an actress. It is hard to overstate how significant Felicity Stoat had been to Hughes. She was the established star, he the 'difficult' playwright. She charming, he truculent and defensive. She the familiar face from television and film, he the 'bargain-basement Beckett'. Now it is Stoat who is forgotten, while Hughes is, if not widely remembered, in the canon. I wonder how much of this is due to Lady Lovilocke's capacity for evisceration.

Many consider Felicity a talented actress, but how many parts can you play if you have no natural smile? Humphrey Bogart got away with it. His smile looked like he was trying to pass something that couldn't be readily expelled. But a strained smile is so much less becoming in a woman.

Felicity seems to labour under the misapprehension that Harauld can be provoked into tenderness. Derision, I've found, serves as neither carrot nor stick. And Harauld, with his keen sense of justice, was unable to brook any unmerited slight. He demands evidence, often written. Were one to say that he had been 'completely insensitive', he would think nothing of arguing for two hours in order to get one to concede that 'almost completely insensitive' might be nearer to the mark.

There are those who find Felicity attractive, and I suppose Harauld must have been among their number, at least when he was very young, almost a boy. But Felicity lacks the capacity for reciprocal flourishing.

She certainly registers on the screen, but her unprocessed hatred gives her a rigidity which prevents the audience from getting truly close. She excels at playing spiteful, shrewish

103

women. She has decent legs and walks well, in a bustly sort of way, though any sensuality is rather subordinated to the unchecked aggression that besieges her so and dampens the corners of her mouth with bubbling pools of saliva whenever she speaks. To be truly feminine, one needs a softness that so many of today's women abhor, and in this, by which I mean this abhorrence, Felicity is a forerunner. These days, there is no baby in the bathwater, for the woman must take her bath first, soaping herself while baby is wailing, unhappy, and spoiling the man's supper!

What remains remarkable is Lady Lovilocke's studied refusal to feel the barest pity for Stoat. By any estimation, Stoat had been ill-used. Lady Lovilocke and Hughes's affair was devastating for her, to say nothing of its effect on their son, Bartholomew, a sensitive boy who struggled to secure a sense of himself in that undulating pool of his parents' narcissism. A pool now awash with the effluent of infidelity. But Lovilocke's diary is an inventory of self-justification:

July 3rd, 1976

Wonder whether to tell the children. Will have to track them down first. Where on earth do they *go* during the holidays? I hope they make it back for Christmas.

Harauld: I think Felicity might be having a breakdown. It's so hard to tell because she's always screaming. It creates the illusion of consistency.

Spoke to Mother – never a good idea. The mention of anything upsetting recalls some greater injury that she has experienced, and the cork of her heart bobs upwards on such a swell of self-pity that she turns her head away, stricken. I have learned, like my siblings, that it is best to distract Mother from anything that might recall her to sadness. We know how to be entertaining, outrageous, ceaselessly irreverent. But what of our own sadness?

Langley: So, are you in love?
Me: Yes.
Langley: Are you sure, this time?
Me: Yes.
Langley: Well, he's a dashed decent playwright. And a hell of a badminton player.

He asks whether I think it'll pass. I tell him no. He raises an eyebrow. 'I see.' But does he?

Why doesn't he fight for me? Not that I want him to make a fuss. Still, I can't help but feel offended.

LATER:
Langley went into a rage and tore strips off one of the children for calling the home telephone without an agreed appointment. Perhaps he does care!

Harauld said he's going to throw himself into this screenplay. I worry. How can he concentrate when Felicity continues to deteriorate so performatively?

Stoat's deterioration was hardly performative, though. She continued to decline and would die by her own hand a few years later, at the tender age of fifty-four, something Lady Lovilocke called 'a final discourtesy, and the wrongful assertion of dominion over God's creation'; Harauld's son Bartholomew did not allow his father to attend the funeral, despite Hughes offering to cancel another engagement and make the dispiriting trudge up to Manchester, where her interment took place. For much of her troubled life, Stoat insisted that she was from the North, and to the North she returned. A distant, more primitive land, in whose spiky soil one hopes she has found final rest. Hughes must have known the effect of his actions on Stoat. I wonder whether, on an unconscious level, he took revenge on Stoat's behalf by killing his own gift.

———

- I would like to talk to you a little about Hughes as a screenwriter.
- Oh. Whatever for?
- How do you feel his work for the screen compares to his work for the theatre?
- Hughes was a playwright.
- Yes.
- And a poet.
- Do you like his poetry?
- I prefer the plays.
- I think I do too.
- And I prefer the poetry to the screenplays.
- Ah.
- Need we say more?
- Well, it might be worth saying a *little* more.
- What would you like me to say?
- I suppose I would like to talk about the films, and how they figured in his life.
- Hughes and I didn't discuss his films. They weren't *from* him.

– What do you mean by 'from' him?

– Just that. They weren't original works. They were jobs for
hire. Would you ask a carpet fitter about how putting down
some underlay 'figured in his life'?

– If I were interested in carpets, I might.

– But you're not.

– Not particularly.

– So you can understand my position.

– Hughes once said:

I refer to my notes.

– 'Adaptation is an art and is no less legitimate a craft than the
writing of so-called "original" screenplays. The joy of adapting a novel into a film is that it allows me to take a break
from one part of my imagination, the part that throws up
these torrential visions, visions that scream, "I'm a play,"
and demand to be given form, and to focus on the part of
my mind devoted to structure, revision and distillation.'

– And now you have read it out.

– You also seem reluctant to talk about Hughes as screenwriter.

– My dear boy, I'll talk about whatever you like. What I can't
do is feign interest.

– What is your favourite Hughes film?

– I don't regard them as 'Hughes films'. They were almost all
directed by Ibssen Anderssen, for a start. They're as much
his films as Harauld's.

– Do you have a favourite film that Hughes wrote?

– Hmm. Probably the one that wasn't made. That's not a joke.

– I know. You mean *O Bedlam! O Bedlam!*

– Plane! shouts Dan.

Wiggsy shakes his head. I mouth the word 'Sorry', as if the plane noise has been caused by my digestive system.

– Back in the room, announces Wiggsy.

I hear Tony Camera's first word of the day:

– Rolling.

Dan shrieks, 'Action!' but we're not really rolling; it's digital. Tony's just pressed 'record' again.

> – You mentioned *O Bedlam! O Bedlam!*
> – I did.
> – How – sorry if this is an obvious question – has it come to be your favourite film of his, if the film wasn't made?
> – As I came to know Hughes better, he was often generous enough to share things before he finalised them. Despite his reputation he was very open about his writing. Very generous.
> – I very much enjoyed reading your introduction to the screenplay.
> – Oh, that silly thing.
> – Not at all – it made me long to read the screenplay.
> – There was a brief moment when it seemed that Harauld would allow the script to . . . resurface, but alas . . .
> – And he let you read *Bedlam* before the shoot?
> – Oh, yes. Every draft. It kept evolving.

———

In *Herstory*, Lady Lovilocke speaks of Hughes's uncharacteristic openness during the writing process:

> Harauld was not one of those dreary writers who guard their work, like those self-righteous types at school, arms crooked into fleshy dams round their desks, as if to stop their brilliance from sluicing out. A hallmark of genius is the self-assurance that it cannot be copied, no matter how much we mortals might wish to partake of its glories. Genius does not begrudge sharing its fruits; it does so freely and without fear. During the writing of *O Bedlam! O Bedlam!*, I had a front-row seat for the best show in town.

– What was especially wonderful was that Harauld's pages – his pages of writing – were filled with notes, sketches and snatches of dialogue, rendered runic by the raised rings of recently dried condensation from his whisky tumbler. 'Ignore the notes!' he would say.

– Do you still have a copy of the screenplay?

– Oh, no. Harauld would hold the draft as I read.

– He held it?

– Oh, yes. He wouldn't let me just *go off with it* . . . It was his.

– And you could concentrate on reading it while he was there?

– You got used to it. And although I know it all got fouled up in the execution, I do believe that that scenario was the absolute equal of his plays, which, of course, places it in the first rank of world literature.

– Each of Hughes's previous scenarios, up until the *Bedlam* script, had been an adaptation. Were you surprised that he would consider writing an 'original', that he would give so much of himself to a medium that is, necessarily, collaborative and – perhaps – given to the dilution of the author's original intention?

– Harauld abhorred dilution. Whether in writing or whisky. Hughes required everything to exist in its most concentrated form. He gave all.

But can one 'give all' to a screenplay? A form which is little more than a promissory epistle, a piece of scrap paper penned in the hope that it might show the way to something substantial, but without the capacity to contain that substance within itself? Might not the mental demands of such a necessarily speculative endeavour weigh too heavily on Hughes's precious store of hope? For Hughes, hope was not a vague yearning, it was the whole thing. And, if his hopes were dashed, might he not be dashed with them and fall, fatally, into a chasm of despair? This was certainly Lady Lovilocke's concern. She simply couldn't understand why a writer of Hughes's calibre would waste an original idea on the cinema. She wrote the following in a suite in Claridge's, as both their affair and the conception of *Bedlam* were gathering pace . . .

Oct. 15th, 1976

'If it's an original, why not develop it for the stage? Then it's yours.'

'I don't want to adapt. I'm tired of film being parasitic.'

'Yes. The concept of cinema as an ancillary art is so terribly draining.'

'You're very beautiful when you're facetious.'

'And when I'm not?'

'Also very beautiful.'

'So perhaps I'm just facetious.'

'And beautiful.'

We ask the staff to run out for croissants and extra eggs and champagne. We'll be hungry in the morning.

Harauld and I continue our conversation on the terrace. The sunlight is beautiful and gives Harauld's sideburns a fetching amber tint. He must have eaten six or seven eggs.

'I insist that whatever I do in film from now on be original to the medium.'

'*Sui generis.*'

'You know that's why I never went to Cambridge?'

'You were too yourself?'

'I didn't have the Latin.'

'What has been will be again, what has been done will be done again; there is nothing new under the sun.'

'Whoever said that hadn't heard of cling film.'

We almost find it funny, don't we, that someone as literate as Harauld wouldn't have been to Oxbridge, but there you have it. There are plenty of people in the theatre who haven't been to Oxbridge, working in junior roles, and many of them make a perfectly decent fist of it.

Harauld was *tired* of questions as to why he had not turned his talents to an original screenplay. 'Loved the last film, but will we ever see an original from you?' a journalist would say. Hughes was sympathetic to journalists. As far as he was concerned, they should be treated like people, but this line would enrage him. 'All my screenplays are original,' he would thunder. And were the offender dim enough to press the matter ('But you know what I mean,' or something similar), the poor wretch would have his head taken clean off. For Hughes, the insinuation was clear, and he resented it. He once said, 'They think I'm incapable of writing an original screenplay. They think all I do is write brilliant words.

Brilliant words are the by-product of what I do. They are the excretion. They're the juices that leak onto the drip tray.'

It was certainly true that Harauld's work was terribly visual. One need only think of the stunning staging of *Flight*, with that marvellous ladder, or the large table in *Table*. And the prologues to his television programme, *The Harauld Hughes Half-Hour*, were like miniature motion pictures in and of themselves. But television is a writer's medium. Film is another country.

––––––

– Do you think Hughes's mistake with *Bedlam* was to try to write an original? That what he saw in his head was too hard to put on the screen?

– Harauld didn't believe in mistakes. He was extraordinarily sensitive, like a speared lion, but unlike the stricken king of the jungle, he knew his weakness was also his strength. He wrote from his wound. We must remember his poem, 'The Wound':

> How wide would
> You say the wound
> Is?
> How red is the blood?
> Has it started to
> Darken?
>
> Can the wound be
> Touched?
> How open is the wound?
> Does it gape?

(I measure it now
With my tongue.
I taste the hurt
And swallow it.)

I would rather you didn't
Do that.
(With the tongue?)
Yes. Or any other part –

(Of my body?)

Yes.

(You must give it
Time.)

I do not have time.

(You must let it
Breathe.)

I cannot breathe.

(You must let the air
Get to it.)

There is no air.
There is no ground.
There is just the wound.
It will not close.
I won't allow it.

(From *The Wound, the Woods, the Well:
The Collected Poems of Harauld Hughes
1957–1977*, published by Faber & Faber)

I allow a respectful End-of-Poem Pause.

– Had the film been made, do you think it would have
  equalled the best of his stage work?
– That is hard to tell. Based on the screenplay, yes. But so
  much of the success of a film relies on the *mise en scène*.
  Though *Bedlam* certainly had a better director than the
  other films.
– Leslie Francis?
– Yes. A theatre man, fundamentally, he had some success
  on the screen – although he didn't in the end succeed in
  making much out of *Bedlam*.
– Why was Leslie Francis the director of this, when all the
  other films were made by Ibssen Anderssen?
– It was completely different to Harauld's other work for The
  Anglers.
– Some of our viewers may not know who The Anglers are.
  Would you mind explaining who they were, and could you
  also incorporate that question in your answer?
– I see. The Anglers were a production company. A film
  production company, always changing their name for tax
  purposes – Anglers Inc., Anglers Ltd, The All-New Anglers
  and so forth. They were owned by Colin and Mickie Perch.
  And The Anglers – it was Harauld who gave them their
  name – made exploitation films. And Hughes, for various
  reasons, became contracted to them. To write some of these
  exploitation films.

He speaks about this as if it were an indecorous family secret.

– Can you tell us what you mean by 'exploitation films'?

— Well, I'm no expert, but an exploitation film is one that
seeks to 'exploit' a theme or a type of behaviour or a subject which will be likely to draw an audience. They are
cheap films that cannot rely on big stars or high production
values, so instead they promise sex or violence or horror or
some other manner of tawdriness . . .

— How is that different to genre films?

— I couldn't care less. I detest the Commercial Cinema. And
in that, I am an ally of Leslie Francis. *Bedlam* was not an
exploitation film. It was to be the first truly *Hughesian* film.
So it needed a director who knew Hughes's original work –
his theatre work, the work that was *him* – and that was
where Leslie came in.

————

Augustus Pink has long been intent on policing the bor-
der between his conception of the Pure Artist, whose work
springs from some mysterious inner source, and that of the
Commissioned Artist, whom Pink regards as little more than
a tradesman, manufacturing words in response to the market.

I am aware of the demarcations The Artist might draw between
work for Them and work for Himself (forgive the male tilt, but
we are talking about Hughes here). Work for Them compels The
Artist to dissociate, because Their idea of Him may not be something The Artist is willing to accept. The Artist must arrange the
sale of what looks like Him to satisfy the buyer, but is in fact
only a part of Him – and not so much that there is nothing left
of Him after the sale is complete. Faust got it wrong. The sale of
one's soul isn't a one-off deal. It's daily. The soul must be scraped,
a section at a time, as with a skin graft, in the hope that sufficient

new tissue regenerates to facilitate future transactions.

Hughes lived in a large townhouse in St John's Wood, he ate at restaurants at least three times a day, enjoyed rare wines in great quantities, dressed impeccably and, when in a hotel (he could nap only in hotels), insisted on a suite. If integrity were lucrative, might we keep it under closer guard? Why should we judge Hughes more harshly because of the scale of his talent? Can we truly comprehend the temptations, financial or otherwise, that beset The Artist of Remarkable Ability?

And might not The Artist of Remarkable Ability reveal himself as much in commissioned work as in the work he instigates? Further, can The Artist of Remarkable Ability do anything other than reveal himself, regardless of how base the form? What *is* this modern obsession with originality? Shakespeare never came up with a plot in his entire life; he was essentially a rewrite man. And did any of the great Renaissance painters choose their own subjects? There must be more to life than crucifixion, but you wouldn't think it by flicking through their portfolios. Can it be a surprise, though? Just look at the receipts. We've all had a difficult boss; theirs was infallible.

———————

— There was another reason for Leslie directing, Pink continues. Ibssen became . . . unavailable.
— I didn't know that.
— Oh, really? What *do* you know?
— How did Ibssen become unavailable?
— Oh, you never heard? I'll leave that one to Mickie Perch.
— Well, yes, we are going to interview Mickie Perch this afternoon.

– How thrilling. Do send him my warmest regards.
– What do you feel about Mickie?
– Mickie is Mickie. He has a worldview that is . . . shall we say *sui generis*?

These tautologies are curtailed by the sound of Handel's *Messiah*. As a ringtone. There are few faux pas while filming, but this is one of them. I've been on set when someone's testicle dropped out of their underpants in the middle of a shot. No one mentioned it until the cast and crew screening, when the actor in question muttered a feeble 'Thanks for that.'

Pink's mobile is in a leather pouch. He unbuckles a securing strap.

– I knew something in there was making a noise. Hello! Augustus Pink speaking.

Whoever's calling knows this. A beat.

– I am, as a matter of fact, with them now. I think they're just leaving. Exactly.

I see his eyes darken. I wonder whether this can be caught on camera or whether it's an effect heightened by my adrenal glands.

– I'm going to have to ask you to leave.
– Oh. Why?
– Not that it's your business, but I'm having lunch with Virginia.
– I thought you hadn't spoken to Harauld since 1977.

117

– Indeed. There will be much ground to cover.

Pink's tone is a fair few degrees below zero. Dan's mouth hangs open. I can see a piece of gum wadded between his cheek and a golden molar.

– You're joking, mate, says Dan.
– I am neither joking nor your mate, says Pink.

The retort is final. The Chardonnay is recorked.
Lovilocke has kiboshed our colloquy.
In his introduction to *Platform*, Augustus Pink writes:

I interviewed Hughes several times throughout his career. He was a tough man to pin down, whether in conversation or on a judo mat. [. . .] He simply couldn't understand why anyone would think they could find out what someone else thought by asking questions.

Perhaps I was foolish to expect sympathy simply because Pink had so often been in similar straits. Our actions are more determined by the roles we play and the positions we occupy than we care to admit. In the role of interviewer, I am (perforce) playing attack; it's only natural that Pink would play defence.

As we pack up and carry the kit to the van, even Wiggsy struggles to minimise our setback. Dan is stress-scratching his hair.

Without this interview, what do we have?

8

ANGLING FOR ANSWERS

[. . .] what is more enduring than the image
of a beautiful woman? Apart from, perhaps,
the memory of one?

From Harauld Hughes, Introduction
to *Harauld Hughes: The Models Trilogy*,
published by Faber & Faber

When we arrive to meet Mickie Perch at his South Suffolk
mansion, his third wife tells me he's just had a stroke. I stand
at the bright-pink door and look back at Tony Camera, who,
instincts honed by twenty years on *Homes Under the Hammer*,
has already panned over to catch my reaction. Dan does the
finger loop for 'keep rolling'. Wiggsy Sound's 'Archbishop of
Banterbury' T-shirt is brined with sweat. Because we've shown
up unannounced – or 'gonzo', as Dan terms it – Wiggsy's using
a boom microphone attached to a long pole held high above his
head, and I can see the matted tussock of belly hair overhanging
his combat belt.

– Today? I ask.
– Just now, she says.

Her cigarette breath funnels in the afternoon light. She
doesn't tell me her name is Candy Doors, but her name is
Candy Doors and she played 'Lavs' in *The Glowing Wrong*, the
last film Harauld Hughes scripted before the debacle of *Bedlam*.

A decorative dog worries her ankles, its tail whipping the smoke into contesting currents.

— Is he okay?
— How should I know? The ambulance took him.
— You didn't go with him?
— Does it look like I went with him?
— Do you know which hospital he's in?
— The nearest?
— Did he tell you I was coming?
— He doesn't tell me anything. Apart from how one day I was going to give him a stroke.

I see a man in the background. He's wearing a short kimono. Or maybe he's just big and the kimono is normal size. The kimono is clearly hers. Everything racks into focus: poor old Perchie hobbles back from a lunchtime sharpener at the village hostelry to discover Candy and the Big Guy slaking their lust in a priapic tangle. In the breakfast nook, of all places (if they have a breakfast nook – it seems like the kind of place that has a plurality of eating stations). Shocked, he keels over, clutching his chest, or wherever you clutch if you're having a stroke (the head?); she calmly dials for the ambulance, before resuming her lovemaking; she doesn't care and neither does her enormous lover; his only concession to the arrival of the paramedics is to throw on one of Candy's kimonos (who cares if it flaps open in the breeze?); as soon as Perch is stretchered into the ambulance, they make love again.

— This is my brother.

A likely story, though they do look similar. Same hungry mouth. He's probably the gardener. D. H. Lawrence knew of what he wrote.

- Are you filming this? he barks.
- We were meant to interview Mickie. About *O Bedlam! O Bedlam!*

Candy tilts her head.

- Well, you're shit out of luck.

She closes the door.

I leave them to their incestuous tryst. I imagine going to the hospital, the nurse asking if I'm Mickie Perch's next of kin. 'Of course I'm next of kin,' I say bitterly. 'I'm his son, aren't I?' And I look down, a single tear stuck in my duct. It wells up but won't fall – I've cried enough for one day.

Dan is down.

- This doc is a write-off.

I ask Dan to stop contracting the word 'documentary' as it's making me uncomfortable (maybe because I respect the form so much?). He continues his monologue:

- The wife is having a family crisis, one brother's had a stroke and the other is on a tropical island.

Colin Perch became a tax exile in Bermuda more than forty

years ago and, in any case, has never given an interview. It is unclear whether he is still alive.

— Mickie was the only one that I wanted to meet. He was the only one who seemed like he had a laugh.

I don't know when, as a society, we moved from 'laughing' to these single laugh units.

— *The Awful Woman from Space* is why I wanted to become a filmmaker.

I had no idea Dan considered himself a filmmaker. I transform my laugh into a cough, but too late for it to sound convincing. Dan tells me that Mickie Perch had already had a stroke earlier that year, while promoting another 'doc' about exploitation film-making called *And . . . Cut!* Dan was in the back of the room at the press brunch, when Perch tipped forward into his overnight oats. Everyone thought it was a joke, but it soon became clear that if it were a performance, something was off with the timing.

We don't even bother to get back into the van. We have nowhere to go.

Dan is disconsolate.

— A two-hour unit move for this shit.

Like he's been trying to shake himself free from a stubborn turd, which is what I feel I've been doing ever since I signed up to this documentary.

Wiggsy lights a joint. When I look at him, startled, he thinks I'm chastising him for not passing it along. I shake my head 'no'. He gives a 'suit yourself' shrug. Tony Camera won't partake either, declaring himself to be a 'white-wine man', which, if you met him, would make sense.

Mickie Perch will die tomorrow. The only publication that will mention it in any detail is *The Echo of the Elephant*:

North Lambeth native, film producer and nightclub mogul Mickie Perch, best known for *The Models Trilogy* and the chain of clubs Mickie's, has died today. His taboo-busting life often placed women at the centre of his films, pushing the boundaries of what he termed 'physical frankness'. Known for his outlandish tastes and bohemian lifestyle, Perch was a key figure in the English exploitation-film scene of the 1960s and early 1970s, producing films such as *The Terrible Witch*, *The Awful Woman from Space* and *The Deadly Gust*.

Perch had two ex-wives and had been engaged no fewer than seventeen times, including to four separate Miss Finlands. He declared himself to be a 'hopeless romantic, capable of falling in love many times a day'.

'Metabolically incapable of fidelity', Perch claimed he didn't count how many women he'd slept with because he hated maths. While asserting that it was tacky to put a number on it, he said in his biography, *Hey Mickie*, that the figure was somewhere in the 'low tens of thousands'. Candy Doors, his last wife, said, 'Mickie was fun and full of life until he died. He loved girls. And it's nice to be loved, even if you know the love isn't specific to you.'

Perch's garish exterior concealed a shrewd businessman and a champion of the arts, having funded the first plays of his half-brother, Harauld Hughes.

9

THE SOUND OF LIGHT

APPLEBY
Julie, baby. You're looking gear. Let
me shoot off a roll.

JULIE
Not now, Appleby. I know you're a top
photographer, but I just want to cool
my boots and rave it.

APPLEBY
I dig that, but I'm all loaded, baby,
and busting to click.

From *The Model and the Rocker* (1968),
scr. Harauld Hughes, dir. Ibssen Anderssen,
published by Faber & Faber

In unscheduled response to this unforeseen rug-pull, we are driving to Kent to meet Miloš Mareck, Leslie Francis's cinematographer on *O Bedlam! O Bedlam!* Unbelievably, Wiggsy installed his jacuzzi. As we step out onto Mareck's pebbled driveway, they greet each other like old friends. Or perhaps they're just old and friendly.

With his long grey hair and explosive beard, there is something folkloric about Mareck, as if he's about to warn you of the dangers of the forest. He seems ill at ease in the living room, where we set up our camera. Among the doilies and china figurines, he's an ageing roadie, back in town to visit his mother. He perches on the edge of the sofa; I wonder if he's been told not to dirty it.

In an article for *Scene and Heard*, Leslie Francis describes his first experience of working with Miloš Mareck:

There was no concern in the voice which asked, 'Is your eye bleeding?'

As the proprietor of the eye under consideration, it was hard to answer with any authority. Indeed, one might venture to suggest that I was scarcely in a position to either confirm or deny the proposition, being in the middle of a field – a carrot field, to be precise – a locale not known for its preponderance of reflective surfaces.

I was directing *Hail to Thee, O Carrot!*, a 'fictio-mentary' (a term of my invention that connotes a poem, in images, on a socially relevant theme, but one freed from the straightjacket of fact), and this particular fugue attempted to interrogate our assumptions about the Humble Carrot Farmer – a figure I'd always held in impossibly high regard, ever since I found out, at the age of sixteen, that nearly all the vegetables we eat are grown by people, and that it could be jolly hard work and terribly tough on the hands, which often become calloused and rough-hewn. The film would start with the sound of children chomping on carrots, while an authentically working-class voice delivered the following verse:

> The carrots are hidden
> Icebergs that cannot melt
> Vitamin'd cones, now orange
> Through Dutch prowess, so they say.
> Tapering, sometimes smoothly
> (Though often not),
> To their apices' blush.

Now, you might think this terribly naive of me, but I was a bookish child, immersed in Homer, Virgil, Lucretius and their ilk, and far along the path that would take me up to Oxford on a full academic scholarship. I was deliriously oblivious of the world around me. I'd been on a bus only once, and that was for a dare; our car was driven by a chauffeur (perhaps he was called Tel or Trev), who idled discreetly nearby if we needed to take a drink in a public house; clothes came from the school shop, casuals from the chap on Savile Row (who must have had a name as well); food was fetched by bicycle by the boy from Fortnum's (who actually was called 'Boy', at least by us) and prepared by Nanny in the downstairs kitchen, before being sent to the upstairs kitchen for embellishments by Chef. Had it occurred to me that my lovely mashed potato, which provided the warmth Mother never could, came from the cold earth, I doubt I could have finished my seconds, let alone my syrup sponge in a custard sea.

'It's gone all red,' continued this steadfast tiller of the soil, the poser of the original interrogative. He was a spirited man, perhaps called Bill, or Brian, or even Clive, and may – for clichés become such because of their frequency of occurrence, not their untruth – have been nibbling an ear of corn. Bernard (shall we call him that?) had lost both his thumbs in a threshing accident, but he still loved to thresh and hated chaff more than any man I'd met. He spat frequently, and with force, and rather placed the onus on those in the vicinity to sidestep whatever he'd expelled. His marvellously big face, lined like a riverbed cracked by drought, was punctuated by a flat cap so time-worn it was mainly air, like tweed candyfloss. He also had a perfectly charming squint. I suppose I loved him, in my own manner, though would never possess him physically. Bernard, you see, was married to Betty, or perhaps it was Letty, and had many children, some of whom had survived childhood, and he was awfully fond of family life, though he could never quite explain why to my satisfaction.

His question had unmanned me, though. How could these agriculturalists trust my theories of montage and composition, how could I be a *metteur en ordre* (as Bresson had put it), a man of command and acumen, when I couldn't even stop blood erupting through my cornea? Bernard motioned to some of his farmer chums, who shambled close, and I recall looking at a crescent of provincial, uncomprehending faces, fuddled by ale and privation. One of them mentioned payment and brought up something to do with the 'boss farmer', and whether he knew about this at all, and whether this was really a film, and if it were a film, when would the girls be showing up? The atmosphere was becoming charged and proletarian and altogether ugly.

My cinematographer, a brilliant Polish man called Miloš, could hardly intercede. He didn't speak a word of English, though he didn't seem overly keen on expressing himself in his native tongue either. A taciturn man, we found our own mode of communication, largely composed of scowls, gestures with the feet and, on occasion, discreet paddles. Having grown up in the ghettos of Warsaw, Miloš would not have thought bleeding from the face unusual, or even worth remarking upon. An unconscionable sybarite, he was relieving himself against the camera tripod. One must not judge a man for his excesses; was it not the bard himself who told us that without the odd indulgence, man is but a bare, forked animal? Abstemiousness can mask a dispiriting lack of zeal. Miloš was not (from the waist up at least) bare, but he was certainly forked and in a state of some distress, emitting noises that would not have been out of place in the jaws of a jackal. It was not without irony, I mused to myself, that it was I who had given Miloš the nickname 'My Third Eye'. Well, My Third Eye was being held down by five farmers and receiving all that East Anglia could offer. I was doubly blinded!

I fell to my knees and began to thrash about, wildly grabbing at any carrot tops I could get a hold of and being perfectly hateful. It was a technique I had learned from the theatre. I was a devotee of Bertolt Brecht, and I knew that, through a considered process of alienating those around me, I would somehow arrive at a powerful truth. Soon it was night, the farmers had long gone, and Miloš slept the sleep of the vanquished. I wiped the tooth dust from his mouth with some carrot tops, removed his day's wages from his back pocket and held him till dawn.

As I stood on the set of *O Bedlam! O Bedlam!*, I frequently felt myself start to fall, like I fell during *Carrot*. However, I knew that were I to so do, I would never get back up again. The people surrounding me weren't farmers. They were technicians, money men, actors and actresses. They didn't have jobs to get back to. This was – as laughable as it seemed – what they did. At the first sign of weakness, the organism, this corrupted body, would expel me. What this meant in concrete terms was that (1) I would be replaced, and/or (2) I would be medicated, and/or (3) I would be sued. These options did not seem amenable, so I carried on, preferring to preside over a disaster rather than pay for one, financially or physiologically. I adopted a mantra, which I muttered incessantly:

> I will not fall.
> I will not fall.
> I will not fall.
> I will not fall.

Mareck is a kindly soul and doesn't lack for geniality. What he does lack is any useful information. A director who made a film every three years might consider themselves active. A cinematographer who makes fewer than three films a year might consider themselves adrift. Mareck has next to no memory of what happened on *O Bedlam! O Bedlam!* Specificity is not his speciality. To him, it's all the same film.

– For me, life is looking. To look is all.

It's a concise philosophy, but one that seems to serve him well.

– I like to shoot.

Another Mareck dictum, and one that shows that, for Mareck at least, perhaps simplicity is all. Cinematographers are visual creatures. For them, the image is what counts. Which can make for memorable tableaux, if not scintillating discourse. I ask him what he thought of *Bedlam*'s script.

– I don't read script. I look.
– How do you know what to film?
– My heart tells me.

Honestly.

– I suppose I was curious to know what the film of *Bedlam* was like. Perhaps you could –
– I did have a script. When we filmed. Now, not filming, no script.

Nothing he says is complicated. That, we must give him.

– Right. But there was a script for the film?

– Of course script. But Leslie doesn't like to give scripts. Script only for Leslie.

He is referring to Leslie Francis.

– And what did Hughes think of that?
– Hughes? Who Hughes?
– Harauld Hughes. The screenwriter?
– I think there were problems. I can't remember. I just shoot.
– So just to recap: you no longer have the script, and even when you did have the script, you didn't look at it because the script was already in your heart, and broadly speaking, you can't remember what you filmed.
– Yes.
– Right.
– I remember some inside, and also fields.

I thank him for his time, though I could have learned more about the film from one of my own dreams.
Dan is down. I steel myself for a post-mortem.

– What's worse than pissing in the wind, Dan reflects, is when the wind blows the piss back in your face.
– I always thought that risk was implied by the phrase itself.
– I'm not talking about the piss going over your trousers – that, you've got to live with – I'm talking about it going in your face and eyes and mouth.
– I see.
– I'm talking about taking a litre of piss in the mouth. That's what that was.
– I get it.

– That was my Saturday.

– I prefer to think of it as 'Saturday'.

– I can't swallow any more piss.

I can't fathom why Dan agreed to make this documentary. He seems resolutely opposed to finding out *anything* about Hughes. The most engaged I've seen him was when Tony Camera mentioned he knew someone who knew someone who might be able to lend us a drone.

Miloš wanders back into the room and offers to help us carry our kit into the van.

– Maybe I have script. Let me check. If I find, I send.

He looks at me.

– I see you. You very sad man.

He steps forward and presses me into a hug that lasts longer than my capacity to resist. It's not that it starts to feel good; it's just that I stop noticing the discomfort.

———————

When we arrive back at the Novotel, there's a note from Miloš. He has been through his files. He cannot find a script for *Bedlam*, but he has found a notebook written by Leslie Francis at the time and is happy to drive down and drop it off, if we can (1) book him a room, and (2) ask Wiggsy if he has the stuff he mentioned.

The words are jagged and the paper is stained, as if Edgar Allan Poe had written an IOU from an abattoir. Ordinarily, what follows might be described as a diary, but as someone equally interested in Zen philosophy, quantum theory and particle physics, Leslie Francis had long disavowed the 'tedious fiction of linearity', preferring to use the term 'thought bullets', with the hope that they might 'ring out for all eternity'.

We join the spree in March 1977, one month before shooting on *O Bedlam! O Bedlam!* is due to start.

THOUGHT BULLETS
by Leslie Francis

Most people are like fish. In fact, we *were* fish once and, to look at the crew on this film, we have not long been out of the ocean. I cannot think above the din of biscuits sloshing in and out of tea. The sounds of slurping and stirring are utterly inimical to high-quality thought. And what else is art but an attempt at high-quality thought? But to even make such an assertion is to open oneself up to the derision of imbeciles.

The correlation between increased individuality and unhappiness is clear. And yet everyone is so awful. Dawning realisation of the impossibility of meaningful interpersonal relationships given the uniformly low-grade thinking of the great mass of people.

I abhor vapidity, and yet I agree to go to the pub with a crew member. Shout someone down for saying that they watch films 'to relax'. Honestly. Why do I bother?

Is intimacy a feasible proposition for one with a revolutionary suspicion of submission? In any case, early start tomorrow. I'll need a big plate of mince to set me up for the day.

Harauld is a miniaturist. His world is a very small one. I don't think he'd even been abroad until he was a Prominent Playwright, cocooned in celebrity, a dull comforter that keeps your own heat in but prevents any exchange. Harauld hasn't really seen the world. The world has seen him.

Harauld's isolation is not that of a great mind; it is of a small soul that erects a barrier around itself for fear that its smallness will be confirmed by those on the outside.

Harauld is insultingly masculine. Example: today I wore my new Norwegian sweater – embroidered, and with ornate clasps on one shoulder. Harauld stops me in my tracks and asks me why the hell I'm dressing like Ibssen. I completely lose my temper. Later, at the hotel, I open all the tins of meat under my bed and put them in the bath and eat like a pig, just with my mouth (no hands). When I open the door to him, my face and hair covered in various foods and juice, he walks past me, sits down on the edge of the bed and just picks up our argument from where we left off. Then he goes to the en suite for a piss – he must have seen the bath full of tinned meat, etc. – but doesn't even put two and two together. Even when I ask if I can use his shower, he doesn't ask why. He just says, 'Of course,' in his booming voice.

I hate the crew. Careerists, the lot of them, not a poet in sight. All they think about is when can they go home. I tell them not to come tomorrow unless they manage to evolve. Crew took me up on my offer. Total shutdown. Only people to stay were catering. They gave me the rest of the vat and a ladle. Miloš [Mareck] also stayed, but only because too drunk to move. Still – oblivion is a kind of loyalty. Lost trousers.

Mickie Perch now on set full-time. Much of the crew returned. New deadline. Very strict b/c of money lost.

Harauld cannot reassure, he can only probe. Why would
I want to be probed by a man with no tertiary education?
Harauld would never admit it, but he is terribly defensive
about his intellect. I got a scholarship to Oxford and was
asked to stay for doctoral work. He left school at fifteen, and
now we're all having to pay. His is the precocity of the urchin,
the hustler – hence his insistence on the spontaneous nature
of his creation – he dismisses formality – he confuses form
with formula – he is incapable of the rigour that insightful
analysis demands. Bogged down in tiresome, debilitating class
resentments, he subjects us to the ungoverned eruptions of his
subconscious.

Of course, the difficulty with a peripatetic narrative is how
to build tension. One establishes a scene, brings it to its
culmination, but how to bring its energy to the next one if
there's no causation? How to get past the assumption that
one event necessarily impacts all subsequent events without
dissipating energy/momentum? And how like the process of
filmmaking itself! One is with a new group of people, and
over the course of a shared endeavour, a certain familiarity –
even fondness – ensues. But then the film is over. One feels
abandoned. Bereft. Much like the first day at a new prep
school – where one is apt to believe that any motherly intimacy
experienced hitherto was merely a sweetener, an anaesthetising
inducement, for the exile to come.

I reject the term 'story' – an excuse for psychological torture
mitigated by the promise of the proverbial 'happy ending'! A
con! An illusion quelling us into grateful docility. In the Happy
Ending our (subliminally imposed) convictions – ones that
make a virtue of self-sacrifice, abstemiousness, the capacity to
subordinate our humanity to the myth of continual growth –
are recognised and ratified by a gnostic hierarchy. In the

courtroom drama the judge gives the verdict. In the western the sheriff gives the badge to the new gunslinger. In the war film the general gives the medal. One's 'peers' congratulate/venerate stoic submission. One self-selects into servitude. Comforting – what befalls us is down to our own actions. Nietzsche was premature. God is not dead. He's become a franchise. You can't move for these new gods. Only these ones don't create worlds. They just create themselves. Hence MEDIA.

On set. Cameraman (Miloš) approaches:

> Him: What are you thinking, Leslie?
> Me: Well, nothing, now.

Told me I'd been staring for quite a while.

> Me: Isn't that the job?
> Him: What should the rest of us do while you stare?

Took walk. Left the lot of them to finish the scene themselves if they think they know what it means.

And what does Harauld think? Who knows? He won't say. He never will. And this mute abnegation of artistic responsibility is solemnised as 'depth'. Well, it's the shallowest depth going.

Receive a full sit-down lecture from Mickie Perch about 'spending'. To be given a slurred encomium about frugality by someone whose mouth is glistening with prawn juice, his angry nose sniffing the crumbs of cocaine still lodged in his comical moustache, is as close as I've come to seeing Satan. Felicity wanders in, and they start necking! No wonder I can't stop screaming! Screaming is the logical response. I should scream more. So I did. And that's when they hold me down. Because, in this country, having feelings is illegal. Broke free, but ran headlong into one of our background artistes. I realised, as I fell into our cheap set, that this had been the first time I'd felt someone touch my body since my pre-shoot medical examination.

I am back in that field. I am surrounded by farmers.

They do not understand.

They cannot.

They do not know me.

I disconnect.

The sound of rotor blades.

I disconnect.

I'm falling.

I grab for carrot tops.

There are none.

Which is all well and good, Leslie, but what happened? And why? *What film were you trying to make? What was* Bedlam *about?*

10

AN UNFINISHING

The problem with endings is how to start them.

Harauld Hughes

Dan is shaken.

– This won't be easy news, he says, but I need to step away for some self-care.

He has called a production meeting, which means that he has asked Tony Camera and Wiggsy Sound to wait outside the van. Dan's T-shirt-tan line perfectly bisects his arm tattoo of the symbol for pi.

– It's not happening, mate. I'm not feeling it.
– How do you mean exactly?

I say 'how' instead of 'what' because I feel the construction is less aggressive.

– We don't have anything to go on.

In this sea of generalities, I can see no way to shore.

– The key elements won't play ball.
– Right . . .

– We had five days to get this doc in the bag.

He's still saying 'doc' as if it's a word.

– Lovilocke: elbowed us. Pink: schtum. Cameraman: useless. Mick Barrett, the only one who *would* talk, isn't even in the films. Doesn't like films! Wasn't in *Bedlam*. And even if he was, probably wouldn't talk about it out of some kind of respect for *the craft* or something.
– How much of this is a surprise?

But the ball is rolling down the hill.

– We had two outlets for this doc, right?

I suppose it's better than calling it a 'film'.

– UK Arts Online, who gave us some seed money, and the British Film Council, who are doing a re-release of *The Harauld Hughes Half-Hour*. And they assured me that this was the exact kind of content they'd love for the DVD.
– No Blu-ray?
– And, depending on how it went, we could have got some festival play.

Good grief. Tony Camera knocks on the van door. Dan waves him away.

– But last night I get an email from the BFC saying that Mark Cousins is going to interview Lady Virginia Lovilocke for the disc, so they won't be needing anything from us.

I like Mark Cousins.

– And then I get a call from UK Arts Online saying that although they were initially interested, they aren't any longer. 'Why?' I ask. They just say, 'It is not for us to discuss our internal commissioning strategy directly.' I say, 'What *is* your external commissioning strategy?' And they say, 'We don't have one.' 'So it's all in your heads?' I say. And they say that they appreciate the news may not be the news I want to hear. I say, 'No shit it's not the news I want to hear, I'm out of pocket' – I don't want to say how many grand but more than a few – and they say those are the perils of independent production, and I say, 'Don't tell me my profession,' because what do they know about being independent – they're apparatchiks gaming the system, grifting off the illusion that film culture can be made into some kind of national service – and I wait for the next bullshit thing they will say, but they've hung up, and when I think about it, I think they had hung up a long time ago. I don't want to sound like a paranoid, but there is an Oxbridge stranglehold on the media in this country, and if someone at the top doesn't like you, they can choke you out. Her ladyship has phoned round all her big-wig mates and she's killed it. She is also denying permission for us to use any extracts from her book.
– I told you.
– Don't gloat. It's very unattractive.
– I *told you*. You need to get permission!
– She's a lady. I thought she would have – you know – honour. I thought she'd be honourable. She said she would support the doc. She's an aristocrat. Their word is their bond and all that.
– You thought the aristocracy was based on honour?

– It's an honour system!

– That's only for honour bars!

– I always find those stressful. Like, you're forcing me to think about ripping you off.

– No system is based on honour. Every system is based on fear.

– Now you're starting to sound like Harauld bloody Hughes. You're going native, mate. The whole thing isn't right. My feeling is, if we stop now, I can write off Wiggsy's and Tony's time – don't worry, you'll all still get something – and it's not been too big of a loss.

I'm not thrilled with the sound of 'something'. It sounds like not much more than 'nothing'.

– Basically, if we shut up shop now, we can chalk it up as one of those things.

– What kind of thing *is* this?

– It *could* be the casting note. Maybe that's why Lovilocke's got the hump.

– Casting note?

– Yes. For the actress playing Lady Lovilocke.

– You put out a casting note?

– Yes.

– Oh, God. Did you write that down? What you told me? That you wanted someone who looked haughty and cruel?

Dan scrolls through the apps on his phone. He pulls up the 'notes' page.

– 'Haughty/cruel-looking actress (30s/40s) required for role of Lady Lovilocke in high-profile documentary. Posh voice and crooked teeth a plus.' Do you think she might have got wind?

– Why would she hear? It's not like she's connected to the world of theatre.

Tony Camera knocks again.

– What is it?

Tony Camera opens the van door. Tony Camera is sweating. A vein is throbbing in his neck, a neck striated by sun and years of chafing under the yoke of factual entertainment (fact. ent.). His is a face susceptible to crimson flush. At time of recording it is somewhere between dark puce and ruddy plum. His white hair has melted from his scalp, which has taken on the texture of a forgotten potato. A reservoir of resentment has built up over decades at the sharp end of low-budget broadcasting, a dense mass of anguish forged in the furnace of overpacked schedules, skipped lunches and compensatory late-night lagers. Now the dam is breached, frenzied waters surge through the cracks.

– What are you two *even talking about*? he yelps. Honestly. Who do you think you are? You do realise no one cares about any of this? No one cares about why some film that didn't get made didn't get made?

I don't know if he means this documentary or *Bedlam*, but Tony's flow cannot be staunched.

– Why does *anything* not get made? There's no story to it. It just stopped. Everything falls apart. Things Fall Apart.

I wonder if, like me, he's read the book by Chinua Achebe.

– My marriage fell apart. I was never there. I was always somewhere else, thinking that one day, I'd have enough money,
enough security to go back to look my wife in the eye. But
there was never enough, and one day, when I came back
early, she was in bed with the engineer who maintains our
living wall.
– What's a living wall?

I now know it's a vertical vegetated wall system with irrigation.

– What does it matter? He was fucking my wife!

I don't like this crude way of talking about the physical act of
love. I think people have imbibed it from the second-act mid-
points of tawdry melodramas.

– Fuck you! Fuck you both.

It's so unnecessary. The 'both' was implied. Tony is at full
power.

– This whole thing is a joke. Every attempt to tell a 'story' . . .

He does the air quotes wildly, as if impatiently beckoning a
plane to land.

– . . . about an unfinished film is the most self-indulgent,
self-important nothing going. It's entirely parasitic on the
pre-existing interest someone has in something that never

was. How do you satisfy that interest? You can't document what would have been because it didn't come into being. Who knows why anything does or does not happen? Who knows why something is good or not? There is no formula. The kind of truth that is expressed in cinema cannot be expressed in another form, otherwise *there would be no point in expressing it in that form*. You can't write an essay on a poem without people having read the poem. And that's what we're facing. We're talking about a poem that no one has read. Just like there is no 'personal journey' in any of these documentaries. They are, let's be honest, a series of random events – generally interviews – with 'notables' – because they're easy to film – linked by a person to give the viewer the sense of consistency. And how are you meant to 'journey' through the life of a writer? They don't do anything – they don't fight wars or make laws or save lives, they just make shit up! Why are they making shit up? They. Don't. Know. There's not one writer in the world who knows exactly why they're doing it – and that's why this documentary is a waste of time and cannot be finished.

Dan takes stock.

– Well, Tony. You're entitled to your opinion.
– What I'm entitled to, Dan, is my fucking money.

Dan retrieves his wallet from his back pocket. I can't believe how thick it is. It's a leather cube, from which the tongues of fifty-pound notes protrude. He pinches out a wedge.

– There.

He throws the notes at Tony. This is learned behaviour from gangster films. He does the same to Wiggsy.

– Consider this an end to our collaboration.

Wiggsy doesn't 'do' disconsolate. He's already ordered an Uber.

– You do realise the irony of this?

We do. Wiggsy says it anyway.

– We've just made an unfinished documentary about an unfinished film.

This isn't the end. This is the beginning. Well, not the beginning. This is the bottom of the second act. The part where things seem dark and there's no hope. The montage where the hero goes into a bar and asks for the server to keep pouring; he'll tell him when he's done. Where he stumbles home, late at night, to be set upon by hoodlums, who kick him, viciously, in the stomach, right where the stunt co-ordinator has placed the padding. The part of the film where the hero is lost and alone. And the whole point of being lost is that you can't see the way out. But then it gets better. I think. I never can remember. I don't ascribe to the three-act system.

Dan is in the van.

No, I don't want a lift.

I'm on my own.

I'm lost and alone.

146

11

BEDLAM BEGINS

How can you be certain you're not doing the very
thing you claim to be deconstructing? I mean, can
you satirise nudity by showing nudity?

Harauld Hughes

I am on a platform. I am no longer pretending to be on a Journey
of Discovery. I'm at Maidstone East. There are no illusions
at Maidstone East. I'm not sure T. S. Eliot, or even Harauld
Hughes, could take the level of reality on offer here.

I am waiting for the train to Kensington Olympia. I am going
to meet Lady Virginia Lovilocke. She doesn't know that yet, but
I have her address from the call sheet.

I look out of the window. There is no voice-over. There is no
camera crew following me. There is no record of this moment.

In preparation for our encounter, I turn to the penultimate
chapter of *Herstory*:

'Where to start?' When I was a little girl, I would often hear
those words on my mother's lips. She would sigh, smooth away
a stray strand of hair and tuck me into a taxi bound for some
faraway relative, with whom I'd stay for goodness knew how
long. The implication, though her expression was hard to read
at a distance, was, 'Can one *ever* start?'

Harauld was distrustful of causation and questioned it in
his work. But a script must have a start, even if it starts at the
end. Harauld had a film to write. The shoot date had been set:

April's Fools Day, 1977. Who says God doesn't have a sense of humour?

Feb. 17th, 1977

Harauld attacks the page in bursts. He simply can't sit down and write on demand, like a clerk. But when an idea seizes him, it's akin to a squall. There's a change in atmospheric pressure. The heavens darken – like he's sucking the energy out of the ether – a shamanic conjuring – and for all I know, it is. Before this ghastly modern era, artists were seen as magical, in touch with the divine. And, often, its opposite . . . Is Harauld in the grip of the diabolical? Well, I certainly believe in the physical manifestation of evil – it can be frightening to see him so overcome. I'm the opposite. I don't write from my unconscious at all. My recipes come from a highly rational part of my mind, as does my theology. Both require order, good measure and balance to achieve that life-giving flavour. And yet people would have us believe that women are the more emotional/intuitive sex! Harauld is positively schizophrenic. He could play both Jekyll and Hyde without any make-up. The reconfiguration is internal, and radically so. It's rather frightening, but thrilling too. Sometimes he's so changed that when I speak to 'this' Harauld rather than 'that' Harauld, I feel I'm betraying his other 'self'! How different he is to Langley, with his unchanging voice. Even as we embark on our divorce, Langley insists on calling me 'darling' and commenting on how well I look, that 'being in love' seems to 'agree with me'. I wouldn't say it 'agrees' with me at all. It commands me. It compels me and will not take 'no' for an answer. I am in its thrall – utterly!

> Harauld: Only primitives pray for rain. Everyone else knows it'll rain regardless.
> Me: One does not pray for 'something', whether it's rain or anything else. One prays for oneself.

Feb. 20th

Such a blow! Ibssen Anderssen was found dead in his Marylebone apartment this morning. Shouts and screams were heard prior to the neighbours discovering dear Ibby, dead, with a broken neck. There were also reports of gunshots, but the people who reported this were themselves shot before being able to give official testimony.

This is what Augustus Pink was referring to when he said Ibssen had become 'unavailable'. It is distressing to hear that one of the key protagonists in our little drama met such an untimely end, and so savagely. In due course, the second coroner returned an open verdict; the first coroner was found dead in his flat before he had a chance to perform the autopsy. 'Death by mis-adventure', the second coroner wrote on the death certificate, in a hand that did not seem altogether steady.

Ibssen's shabby apartment wasn't split-level, so it's hard to fathom how he fell down so many steps. Mickie Perch was known to have underground connections, and Ibssen was said to have owed him money, having run up debts with dealers of black-market anti-allergy nasal sprays. The story with Mickie was that he would give someone two weeks' grace to clear their debts. After that he would 'make his position clear'. A warning would be issued, then there would be 'an event' or 'accident' from which the Aforewarned would only narrowly escape. If the would-be victim was unwise enough to think themselves lucky, they would not think themselves so lucky next time.

Asked if Harauld suspected foul play, he darkened, and his eyes dimmed to a cold grey.

H: Mickie's my friend.

Me: What does Mickie have to do with it?

H: Ibby was a bloody drughead! It was a matter of time. He was louche. Dangerously bloody louche.

I know it's terribly unfashionable, but I would rather someone be a fall-down alcoholic than have so much as a puff of pot or any of that other rot with which people insist on ruining their temperament. Intoxication is the sometimes perilous by-product of drinking, the price one must pay for something so delicious. But to choose intoxication without the taste of deliciousness seems to me to be so bovine, base and wholly uncivilised as to be demonic.

Feb. 21st

Saw an interview with Mickie Perch in the *Telegraph*:

'Ibssen Anderssen's death doesn't change anything. The Anglers will press on with our next production. Harauld Hughes is writing an original script for us as we speak. A new director will be found.' In answer to the question of whether The Anglers' films are exploitative, Perch replied, 'All film is exploitation. Until the means of producing a film are as cheap as ink and paper, movies are nothing more than a business loan. And I know to make good on my loans.'

The only thing Mickie knows is how to undermine women's understandable reluctance to disrobe on camera.

'Mickie Perch . . .?' I ventured once to Harauld. 'Isn't he just dreadful? Those suits . . .'

One would see photos of him falling out of clubs with cocktail waitresses.

'I owe him,' is all Harauld would say. But I don't have such a transactional view of life. I do not ascribe to an economy of love. But Harauld, I fear, is still trying to clear his debts.

The inference is clear, like a see-through lake: Hughes still hadn't told Lady Virginia that Mickie Perch was his half-brother!

Feb. 22nd

A note from Harauld. 'It is not a debt. It is a bond.'

But the language is still that of economics. It merely transfers the interest from one party to another. It was one of the few things about which Harauld and I would ever have cross words. He was terribly generous, but he knew the cost of everything. I never checked the price tag. Why bother? If the cheque bounces, they'll let you know.

Harauld told me that when he was a struggling young man, Mickie Perch put up the money for *Platform*, the play that launched Harauld onto London's theatrical scene. In exchange, Harauld agreed to write ten film scripts for Mickie.

'Ten!' I exclaimed. 'That's a prison sentence.'

'Ten is Mickie's lucky number.'

'Lucky for some,' I said, with no little rue.

I told Harauld that it might be wise to concentrate on a new play instead. Why write a film at all? Harauld was outraged. 'And betray Mickie? It's unthinkable. I gave him my word. Without my word, what am I?'

'A very handsome angry man,' I said. Harauld liked that.

We were near Holland Park when he told the driver to park the Rolls somewhere discreet and take a long stroll. Oh, we were wicked!

Harauld once told me, 'You're too emotional for cinema. All the tricks of the medium are designed to overcome people's defences, to get them involved. But you're already so deeply involved in life and its meaning. It's like you have no skin.'

'I can't say that makes me sound terribly attractive,' I remember saying.

'Oh, I only like girls without skin,' he said. He was terribly sensual, like a satyr.

But it was Harauld who was about to have his skin taken off, and it wouldn't heal for a very long time.

Feb. 24th

Surprised to hear that Leslie Francis will now be directing Harauld's latest. Such a contrast to dear Ibby. Am I the only one who thought *And . . .?!* terribly unradical?

———————

Indeed, still hot from *And . . .?!*'s triumph at the Berlinale (where it received an honour for the most innovatively punctuated film of the year), Francis was ill-prepared for pliancy. Freshly garlanded as the Saviour of Cinema, he combined the arrogance of a neophyte with the truculence of an old hand. On 21 February 1977, the day after Anderssen died, Francis wrote to Hughes, as if he had been hired previously; as if the death had been expected:

Harauld. Shame about Ibssen, but we mustn't dwell. Re the New Film: I want to make an intimate epic. Whether we like it or not, film can only convey thought via the human face, and the best way to show thought on the human face is to juxtapose it (in montage) with various affecting images. Thus the quest, which perforce takes the hero through a multiplicity of affecting images, has always been one of the most successful story forms; voyage as *ronde*, in which one returns to a home of some sort, older, wiser and with the possibility of a sequel. But the only believable journey I feel we can make is straight to hell. We start in delusion and end in derision; when we flee, it is *into* reality.

In the creation of a shooting script, Francis's practice, in contradistinction to the non-interventionism of Anderssen, was to propose an outline, have a writer 'flesh it out' and then, to continue the metaphor, strip it back to the bone. When the writer was flayed beyond the capacity to continue, Francis would simply hire another one. But Hughes, as we more than know by now, was no mere *writer* . . .

Bedlam would reveal what happens when two intransigent auteurs simultaneously try to make a personal film set to an as-yet-unrecorded Donny Chapel* score. We know it ended badly, disastrously. The question is, how?

Lady Lovilocke continues with *Herstory*:

Feb. 27th

Harauld hard at work; suggested *Bedlam* for the title, in keeping with the titles of his plays, which are nearly always one word (his tendency to compress), but Leslie still very keen on *O Bedlam! O Bedlam!* Says he wants the film to be a ballad, Homeric in scale. 'Homeric? Or oneiric?' Harauld said. People forget how funny he is.

'Spoken like a true philistine,' said Leslie.

Harauld was wounded, terribly.

'Is it philistine to distil?' he asked me, eyes glistening.

Behind the pain, a truth: if Leslie is already repeating himself in the title, how long will the film be?

Me: Why don't you direct *Bedlam* yourself? Leslie has got up himself.

---

* Chapel would eventually release an album, *After Bedlam*, with lyrics by Harauld Hughes. The lyrics are reprinted in *Harauld Hughes: Plays, Prose, Pieces, Poetry*, published by Faber & Faber.

Harauld was appalled. 'That would be a total betrayal.' Harauld is obsessed with honour.

Harauld certainly had the eye of a director and a wonderfully sensitive ear for actors and rhythm, but he distrusted hierarchies. He had no interest in the logistics of moving a large group of people from one location to another. Nor did he have the patience to wait for the right light. Words, yes. Light, never.

> Me: But haven't we betrayed our spouses? And don't we continue to betray them with our affair? We betrayed them again just now, in the walk-in shower, and then on the divan.
> H: That is completely different. To not have an affair would be to betray our own hearts. And without hearts, how can there be honour, for in what would we hold it?

March 2nd

Harauld passed me a note today: 'You are my blood. You pour through my heart. My heart is deluged. My breath is not mine. All best, Harauld.'

March 6th

Shooting on *Bedlam* starts in a few weeks. Felicity, had she any decency, would have withdrawn. But she says she needs the money. Nonsense, of course, as Harauld has already promised her the house + generous settlement. She simply cannot bear to be shut out of anything. Regardless, her part isn't overly large, so one hopes her presence can be contained? But I feel for Harauld, whose relationship with Leslie is already strained. Leslie is terribly loyal to Felicity. Men of his ilk do seem to enjoy the dependence of women in decline.

I wonder whether Leslie is more drawn to the drama surrounding his dramas than the dramas themselves. I hope

Mick [Barrett] or similar will keep Leslie's attention/affection fixed elsewhere . . . Mick is terribly handsome, though given to excess, a typical actor roué. In another life, we might have had an affair, but the attractiveness of brutes, for me at least, withers as soon as you're in their arms. Their hunger, in that moment, for that to which they believe you've surrendered makes them utterly repellent. Such a beast is best appreciated at a remove, like an erect lion prowling on his sun-blanched mesa.

March 8th

Harauld yet to finish the script. In two minds as to the ending. Leslie sent him a stiff letter asking him to 'make up his mind'. I felt terrible. To accuse someone like Harauld of vacillation. I asked him to hold me. He did. We made love. But with less relish than usual. Afterwards, he had his usual fry-up but would only pick at the French toast.

March 10th

Leslie still demanding rewrites, knowing full well that Harauld cannot write unless something erupts from his subconscious.

March 11th

I finally met Mickie [Perch]. I have to say, he is lovely-looking and so polite that it's hard to believe he did all those dreadful things that people say he might have done, such as shooting people and so forth. The air of danger around him is highly arousing – it must be admitted – and Harauld does rather look like Mickie. I hope that doesn't make me prejudiced. I think the similarity goes beyond ethnicity . . . Mickie often looks

at me with something not unlike desire. Though – and I feel
this is the woman's lot – so do most men! I'm not unattractive,
I suppose; it's just never mattered much to me. And Mickie
seems to love many, many women! Has he killed? More than
once? If so, will he kill again? I hope not!

March 12th

Harauld, don't ask how, got hold of the most ghastly letter
from Leslie. When I press him as to its contents, he demurs.
Suffice to say, Harauld made his feelings clear to Leslie. So
clear, it seemed, that Leslie had a small cardiac arrest. I'm
ashamed to say I'm glad.

March 13th

Mickie held a casting session for the film while Leslie
recuperates in his Sussex retreat. Harauld appalled. 'Why are
they only auditioning dancers?' Mickie keeps talking about
how important flexibility is on screen.

March 15th

Harauld back from a casting session.

> Me: Won't you have your head turned by all these beautiful
> actresses?
> H (wailing): Don't be absurd! I'm a boy! I need a mature
> woman. I'm your boy!

It was so terribly touching to watch him howling 'I'm a boy'
over and over as his voice became increasingly hoarse.

Harauld incandescent. Received a STACK of notes from a mostly recovered Leslie. When he opened the envelope, he sounded like he'd been shot. He fell off his chair. An example:

> The line 'Listen to me, asshole' has a danger of sounding like 'Listen to my asshole', which, I have to say, might not be far removed from the experience of listening to the scene, and dare I say, the film as a whole. In the same vein, it's unclear whether 'computer justice' refers to justice administrated *by* computers or justice *for* computers. If there were any justice for *me*, we would cut this scene, though I do like the line 'Computers killed my brother!' Also: is 'the Justice Machine' battery-operated, or can it run off the mains?

The Three Ages of Woman, according to Mickie Perch's costume notes:

Furry bras = Stone Age.
Leather bras = medieval times.
Sparkly bras = the future.

Me: Why don't you tell them to go hang? If they won't make your script, tell them you're off!

Harauld says he's given his word and 'needs the money'. All very unfocused. Something to do with a 'recoupment'. He's worried Felicity is going to 'take the lot'.

Me: I thought Mickie had all your money?
H: He does!
Me: So, what can she take?!
H: The money I'm hiding from Mickie!

I never think about money, which I know is childish. It's just so boring, and it never gets you anywhere. I think worrying about money is a way of rejecting the present and, of course, God. Harauld is in such a state about it. Says he was once poor, and it was ghastly. Also, has come to rely on chauffeur/Rolls, etc. – doesn't want to have to go back to taking public transportation. Imagine, poor Harauld on a bus!

There is a break in my diary here. It represents the time of the shoot for *Bedlam*, which Harauld, as was his custom, attended throughout. I am afraid to say that the pain of being separated meant I was entirely incapable of writing so much as a word. Until what proved to be the last day of principal photography.

May 1st

Awful day. Just awful. Went to set as guest of Harauld. He sweetly arranged for a helicopter to pick me up. Landed during the middle of a take! The scene had something to do with a spider overlord. Harauld said I did everyone a favour by interrupting. Felicity saying the lines like she was a rail announcer. If looks could, etc., etc. After, everyone very stand-offish. Felicity wouldn't even kiss me hello! She looks absolutely ashen. It's pure pride. H and I didn't plan to fall in love. How she can act when her face is so rigid, I don't know.

Leslie (wearing beret!) filming strange scene – discovery of giant spider tentacle. It rather looked like one of those draught excluders you find in the houses of the cash-strapped. I casually mention this to Harauld, I suppose too loud. Harauld howled in appreciation. In fact, it *was* a draught excluder, puppeteered from below!

Leslie called for quiet. Harauld, gallant, told Leslie to be quiet, but using other words.

Leslie asked Harauld if he would like to direct.

H (shouting from his chair): Why don't you give it a go, Les?

No one calls Leslie 'Les'.

Leslie: And what, exactly, is this shit that you're asking me to direct?

Audible gasps. Shifting retreat in anticipation of a one-on-one confrontation.
Harauld standing . . .

H (to me): I'm sorry about this.
Me: I feel just terrible.

Harauld removes his jacket. Carefully folds it and puts it on the chair. He leaves his glasses on.
He walks up to Leslie. Felicity, gaunt and self-involved, intercedes.

Felicity: Harauld. Stop. This isn't right.

Without Harauld to write her lines she's nothing.
Harauld tries to pass her. She keeps standing in his way, thus literalising what she's been doing his entire adult life.
Mickie [Perch] bursts out of a static caravan, looking deranged and trailed by two . . . I don't know what to call them, but neither 'lady' seemed to mind the cold. He must be on drugs. Heated exchange. Mickie, I notice, holding a badminton racket. He starts to swing it. Harauld, effortlessly, catches it and breaks it over his thigh. I feel a surge of attraction. He throws the two pieces away. He walks towards me.
'Harauld!' I cry. But Mickie has already leaped onto his back, and the two are now writhing on the ground, while Felicity looks on, lustily.

H: Look away, Virginia! For God's sake!

I clamp my hands over my eyes. I am in paroxysms. I can hear laboured breathing and the dull thud of blows. I pray: 'Please, Lord, may it be Harauld landing the blows, and not receiving them.' I feel hands on my face. It is Harauld. His nose is bloodied.

H: Let's get to the chopper.

We go. Leslie clambers, pitiably, onto Harauld's back. Harauld doesn't slow; he has carried him his whole life.

'But who will direct? What of Harauld's marvellous script,' I pant (we are running v. fast). Harauld says, 'I'm sorry. But it's over.'

For a moment I worry that he means us. I faint. Later, I awake and look out at the most beautiful sky I have ever seen, suffused with gold. The light catches Harauld's curls, and he appears as if he's an angel. Which, I feel, he is.

I am not dead. I am with Harauld. And we are not over. The film is. We are beginning. We are becoming. We are without ending.

I have fainted again. The violent wind and petrol fumes revive me.

Me: Where's Leslie?
H: He decided to stay with the others.

What a day!

H: Darling Virginia. My love. My angel.

He sees me. Finally, someone sees me. Harauld offers me something from the minibar. I have a delicious Scotch.

Me: But what about the film?
H: The film is dead. Mickie is dead.
Me: Mickie's dead?
H: Figuratively. He's probably gone back to his trailer. I am yours. I was always yours. Mickie knows that now. I will never write a film again. I can't. You are my film. You are the ribbon of dreams that flickers on the screen of my soul. But,

for me, the debt is paid. You know Mickie was my brother? *Is* my brother?

Me: I suspected as much. He's so handsome. But I didn't want to come across as prejudiced. And there's another one, isn't there? Colin? Who I hear is very boring and likes maths.

H: I'm so ashamed. Neither of them read!

Me: But you read, Harauld. You read for all three of you!

H: I read only for you. I will write only for you. I will never write for others again. You are my home. I am free.

Me: You always were free. We are all free. But to know it, we must know we are loved.

Harauld lifts that head of his, sun-fringed into umber, and though I can't be sure, smiles.

We touch down. We are in Holland Park. We are home.

The pilot says we shouldn't really be touching down in Holland Park, a view that seems to be shared by other people in the park, but what do they know? What do they know of our love?

What do they know of Harauld?

But how did Harauld finally pay back his debt? What did he do to free himself from the bond?

12

INTERVIEW WITH A LADY

                    SHE
What's this?

                    HE
It's whatever we want it to be.

                    SHE
It's hardly that.

                    HE
You know what I mean.

                    SHE
I don't. I really don't know what you
mean.

                    HE
It's another room. That's what it is.

                    SHE
Ah. A room. It's a room.

                    HE
Don't start.

                    SHE
Oh, I haven't.

                    HE
Haven't what?

                    SHE
Started.

From *Table* (1961) by Harauld Hughes,
published by Faber & Faber

Lady Lovilocke's housekeeper answers the door. Yes, I do know
this is a private residence. No, I do not have an appointment.
Yes, it *is* urgent. I *am* prepared to wait. I *am* aware that Lady

Lovilocke may not be inclined to see an uninvited visitor. No, I didn't know Lady Lovilocke is asleep. I thought this *was* a civilised hour. I check the time on my phone. It's almost noon.

– Come back two. Two thirty.

She sounds Portuguese. Or maybe she's Spanish and drunk.

Lady Lovilocke's day room has an authority. 'I am as a room should be,' it says. It doesn't look designed, nor does it draw attention to itself; nothing is too new, and if anything is care-worn, it is charmingly so. This room cannot brook banality; it is a place where books are needed, where the life of the mind is sustained, where the sanctity of language is defended. I wonder how much it cost.

Lady Lovilocke wanders in with the distracted air of someone whose presence has always registered, her beehive stacked in soft heaps.

– Where do you want me?

Dan's mental Rolodex of double entendres would have spun off its axis. I stand up and gently wave.

– It's just me. We're not filming.

She looks up. Her hand levers to her mouth.

– Harauld?
– Ah. Yes – people say I look a little like him.
– It's extraordinary. I mean, you have no style – and your voice is terribly thin – but otherwise it's as if he's here.

She peers past me.

— But where's everyone else?
— It's just me.
— I suppose it's all on the phones now? And then straight on the Net, I imagine?
— Normally there are three others, but they're not here.
— Oh, why ever not?
— They . . . gave up.
— But not you.
— Not as yet.
— What was the documentary called again?
— *The Unfinished Harauld Hughes.*
— Ah, she says.
— 'Be careful what you wish for.'
— I'm afraid I'll have to sit. It's my hip. Well, it's not mine — it's just *in* me. Funny — one never thinks to ask where the hip that's replacing your old one *comes from.* But it must come from somewhere.
— I think they're plastic or metal.
— I don't like the idea of that at all. Why can't they use actual bone?

We are sitting underneath an oil painting of Hughes, in badminton whites, smashing a shuttlecock over a net. He liked it so much that he asked the artist to paint another version, which now hangs in the National Portrait Gallery.

— So you want to ask me about Harauld?
— How do you find speaking about him?
— One becomes used to it. I agree with the world — Harauld

165

is very interesting. Where we disagree is that while I regard him as an ever-complexifying mystery, the world would reduce him to a comprehensible set of attributes.

— Why do you think he was so unique?

— I couldn't begin to answer. All I know is that Harauld would have absolutely *hated* that question. Who *isn't* unique?

— I can think of some people.

— Well, you can't know them very well.

— Why did Harauld stop writing?

— Oh, he never stopped writing. He was always writing in his head.

— Right.

— Or perhaps you're one of those people who think that writing only happens when someone is dragging a pen across paper?

— Do you mean he wrote for himself?

— One always writes for oneself. One only writes cheques for others.

— His last play was published in 1972.

— Was it really?

— Did you expect this . . . slowing down in his productivity?

— What a ghastly word. 'Productivity.' How industrial. How mercantile.

— But we are sitting in a room filled with books, produced on a mass scale, for public consumption.

— Something isn't real unless it's for sale. Is that the point at which we've arrived?

— I don't think that's quite what I mean.

— What is it that you *do* mean?

— Well, as an admirer, I miss his writing.

— And, as his wife, I miss *him*. All of him.

166

Her moistening eyes are making micro-adjustments; her ruched eyelids redden through their faint dusting of peach. I try another tack:

— I wanted to ask specifically about *O Bedlam! O Bedlam!*
— Why would anyone want to talk about that?
— Because it seems to represent a point of no return.
— To what would he have returned?
— Well, writing screenplays, writing plays.
— He was very disappointed with how *Bedlam* went. That much is true. Yes, he never really recovered from that particular exorcism. But if you're interested in all that, you should read my book.
— Oh, I am. I'm reading it now. I'm rereading it.

I search for the book in my rucksack. I hold it up, like a Boy Scout with a merit badge.

— Well, it's all in there. There's nothing else to report.
— You don't really write about the film as such.
— How could I? I wasn't there. That was the era when wives weren't invited. Wives were expected to stay at home and *occupy* themselves. Wives weren't meant to get in the way.
— Unless the wives were actresses.
— What do you mean by that?
— Well, Felicity Stoat was his wife at the time. And she was there. She was acting in the film.
— Felicity wouldn't give Harauld a divorce. That was the only reason they were still married. They had been living separate lives for years.
— But they had a son.

167

— The son was gone by then. He was a grown man.

— What happened to Bartholomew? Do you see him?

— These are very personal questions.

— I'm sorry.

— What do you hope to gain from this kind of intrusion?

— I suppose an understanding.

— The kind of understanding that comes from pinning someone down?

— I'm not trying to pin you down.

— Are you sure? How do you know?

— I hope I'm not.

— I do not see Bartholomew. He works in finance. It's all very painful. He doesn't read.

— He can't read?

— Of course he can read! He just chooses not to. That was his way of hurting Harauld. He rejected all literature. He just earns pots of money and watches sport.

— But Harauld liked sport.

— Harauld liked badminton. He *hated* sport.

— I see. So you didn't write about *Bedlam* because you weren't there.

— Yes. I presumed my being there would be a prerequisite to my being able to say what being there was *like*. You seem to be harping on about matters you have barely heard about.

— But I imagine you spoke to Hughes during the production?

— I dare say I did.

— But you didn't feel able to write about it?

— I wondered whether it was my place. And I barely spoke to Harauld. It was a dreadful time, the longest separation we've ever endured. Until the one I'm enduring now.

— Why did you speak so little during *Bedlam*?

– He was writing.

– During the shoot?

– Yes.

– Rewriting scenes?

– Harauld didn't rewrite. He wrote.

– But what exactly was he writing during the shoot?

– The script!

– Why?

– Because there was no script.

– There was no script? How do you mean?

– What do you mean, how do I mean?

– I mean, you need a script.

– That's what Harauld thought. Which is why he was up every night writing one.

– So . . . I mean, why didn't he . . . I mean, was it planned for it to be written so late in the day? I mean, so close to production?

– No. It wasn't.

– So what happened?

– Harauld had written a script, a very brilliant script, but Leslie rejected it. Harauld was terribly hurt, of course, so he destroyed it.

– The script.

– Yes. The script. He could hardly destroy Leslie. He demanded his copy of the script back – you were never allowed to read a script of Harauld's unless he was physically holding it – and he tore it up into minute little pieces and ate it. Right in front of Leslie. Very slowly. And, of course, that put everyone's backs up. Because all this was about a week or so before the shoot. So Leslie told him to start writing again. And Harauld simply said, 'I can't. I'm full.' So Leslie said they would have to make something up. And Harauld said, 'I just made something up. You didn't seem to like it. So why don't *you* make something up, and I'll see what I think of that?' So Leslie went away and gave him an outline.

– But Hughes was unable to work to an outline.

– Not so much unable as constitutionally opposed. It was a fatal combination, really. Leslie was developing all these notions. Like actors couldn't play characters. They could play only themselves. And to be fair to Leslie, when you look around these days, you'd be hard pressed to disagree. So characters were out. The script had to be moulded to the actors. Well, that wasn't how Harauld worked at all. When he wrote, the characters were called 'Character A', 'Character B', 'Character C' and so forth. He never *described* a character in his life. He felt that was terribly restrictive. Controlling. The character told *Harauld*. Harauld could listen to a character. He certainly couldn't listen to an actor or an actress. An actress's only real topic of conversation is how no one sufficiently appreciates her. That is the basis of a diatribe, not a drama.

– There are some who say that Harauld's female characters were based on Felicity Stoat – that she provided a model for them – and that perhaps, without her to base his characters on, he wasn't able to write.

– I wonder why others weren't similarly inspired by Felicity. After all, she was around. Very much around. Any similarities in those characters were the outworking of her incapacity to expand past her own limitations and Harauld's generosity in ignoring them.

– How did you feel about Harauld going off to be on a set with his wife?

— Your question seems to contain its own answer.

— May I read you a quote from Leslie Francis about Hughes?

— You seem to be unfolding the paper . . .

— 'Harauld's surrealism is, at base, anti-humanist. For it accepts, unquestioned, the random and possibly disordered firing of neurons as the basis for the communicative act. Where is the depth?'

— Well, that was Leslie. His idea of depth was to have a framing device. That, for him, gave things another level. But it just takes you further away from the picture. Or, as Harauld put it once, 'Leslie is more frame than picture.' Leslie always had to *show you* he was making the film. That anything else was dishonest. You had to reveal the hand that was doing the magic trick. I rather feel magicians should keep their hands under the velvet tabletop, where we can't see them. Harauld didn't believe in magic. Is there anything more detestable than a magician? Harauld was more like a prophet. A blessed messenger bringing back something, unbidden, from another dimension.

— What happened when it came to the actual filming? Did they have a story?

— No. They had some songs, for which Harauld had written the lyrics. And I believe they spent some time filming Donny Chapel and the Chatterers performing those songs. I think they thought that would buy them some time. In any case, each evening Harauld was locked in a room with a typewriter, and he just had to come up with something. Whatever he came up with in the night – well, that's what they shot in the morning. And, of course, you can imagine what this did to his spirit. The pressure. The strain – to conjure up three or four scenes every night. From which Leslie would choose one or two, or none, as the spirit moved him. Harauld hoping that they would eventually cohere. That a thread could be found. And Leslie would say, 'Well, if it ever gets confusing, we can cut to a song or we'll just write ourselves in. We will play ourselves *not being able to think of anything*. We will *discover* the film, and even if we don't discover it, we will *document* our failure to discover the film.' That was always Leslie's strategy. Show yourself. But art must move beyond self-portrait, no? Especially if the self-portrait is of an artist who doesn't know what the hell he's doing.

— So when people mention that there's a script of *Bedlam* in a Swiss vault, what are they talking about?

— I have no idea. Perhaps there are some pages, some suggestions for the day's work. But there is no script. There is no real *film*. Just scenes. And screen tests. Endless screen tests. Harauld once thought he could . . . how to put it . . . remember what he wrote. He was going to write it up. Not rewrite, recall . . . Augustus Pink wrote a foreword . . . It was all ready to go . . . but he couldn't remember. It had dissolved.

My white whale is a sprat.

— How has this been kept . . . hidden?

— You're involved in television, aren't you?

— On occasion.

— So you probably don't know what it's like to be part of an artistic endeavour. In an artistic endeavour of the kind that one might undertake on a Harauld Hughes production, a certain privacy is required so that creativity might flourish.

– You say a Harauld Hughes production, but *Bedlam* was a
  Mickey Perch production.
– It was an Anglers production.
– Which was Mickie's company.
– His and Colin's company.
– Yes.

I give a decorous half-bow.

– I should say, sorry for your loss.
– What loss?
– Mickie Perch. He died . . .?
– Did he?
– Oh. I'm sorry. I thought you would know . . .
– Maria! Maria!

Disconcertingly, Lady Lovilocke does not avert her eyes from
me. It is as if I have become Maria.
Maria appears at the door.

– Did you know this?
– Did I know what, miss?
– Mickie Perch has died.
– He died? How?
– I've absolutely no idea. How did he die?

I answer. She turns to Maria.

– A stroke.

Maria crosses herself . . .

– I hope it hurt.

. . . and walks out.

– I'm presuming you were not in touch with Mickie.
– I was not.
– When did you last see him?
– When did I last see him? I last saw Mickie Perch on the last day of shooting before *Bedlam* was abandoned.
– When Harauld kicked him away from the helicopter?
– Yes. How did you know?
– I read your book.

Were this a game of Hughes's beloved badminton, you might say that this is the point where it becomes a proper rally.

– Well, that – to quote Harauld – 'somewhat reconfigures matters'.

Lady Lovilocke explains that Harauld didn't really kick Leslie out of the helicopter; he had shrugged Leslie off somewhere before the helipad.

– Yes. Are you sure Mickie's dead? He never struck me as the type of person who would accept death. Can the undead die?
– What do you mean?
– A private joke, I suppose. We called Mickie 'The Vampire'. He was the most purely parasitic man I've ever encountered. He took, but only at your initial invitation.
– And what of Colin?

– Colin died a long time ago.

– Oh. I didn't know.

– No one knows. No one really knew him. It was all rather sad.

– What happened?

– What happens in any family? Various interests come into conflict, no one has the humility to back down, things fall apart. Do you know Achebe?

– Yes.

– Good. You see, they didn't have a mother. And how can you live without a mother? Or rather, how can you learn to live without a mother to show you how to live?

– What were the various interests?

– Don't you know by now? Goodness me. What have you been doing in this documentary of yours? Who have you spoken to?

– Mick Barrett. Augustus Pink. Miloš Mareck. That chap from the Archi(v)tèque.

– Simon?

– Yes.

– Useless. Anyone else?

– No. We were going to speak to Mickie, but he was already dead. Well, he was pronounced dead at the hospital.

– So, essentially, you've spoken to four ancient men.

– Yes.

– No wonder your friends gave up. I presume they were middle-aged men like you.

– Yes.

– Heaven help us.

– We *wanted* to speak to you.

– Well, I'm here now.

– You said Mickie's death 'reconfigures' matters. In what way?

– Harauld was very loyal.

– Yes.

– And there was a certain code that existed between Mickie, Colin, Harauld and Mickie Two.

– And what happened between Harauld and Mickie? Did kicking Mickie out of a helicopter constitute a breach of the code?

– Not in the slightest. Adherents of the code were not prohibited from inflicting injury on each other. Such is the risk of engaging in bundles and surprise attacks and so forth. No – the code had already been broken.

– And who broke the code?

– Mickie, of course.

Without meaning to, I slow down, as if something dreadful might be revealed.

– How did Mickie break the code?

– Mickie, it turned out, had been having an affair with Felicity.

– I see.

– I'm obviously aware that Harauld was having an affair with me. That was completely different. That did not cut across any lines of allegiance within the group. It did not break the code. What Mickie did was a complete betrayal.

– How long had the affair been going on?

– The scandal of it all is that Mickie and Felicity had been having an affair since before Felicity met Harauld on the platform.

– So they did meet on the platform?

– I'm using 'platform' figuratively, like Harauld did. Of course, there was no platform – but it's passed into myth. They met on *Minions of the Moon*. I wrote about this. But it was a long time ago. This is old ground. You see, before Felicity and Harauld met, she had been having an affair with Mickie. But then Felicity had affairs with everyone. And I think they may have broken it off a little when she took up with Harauld, but pretty soon she took it up again.

– Took up what?

– Mickie. So, from the start, Mickie had been betraying Harauld. Which, if you think about it, puts everything into doubt. And then there's a twist.

– The affair with Mickie wasn't the twist?

– No. The affair with Colin is the twist.

– Colin? I thought Colin was a celibate.

– Not when Felicity was around.

– And when did Colin start his affair with Felicity?

– Just after Felicity started her affair with Harauld. But Colin didn't break the code.

– How is that not a breach of the code?

– Colin had no idea about Felicity and Harauld. Felicity was spinning those boys like plates. And as soon as Colin found out about Felicity and Harauld, he cut her off. He never recovered. Broke his heart. And when he found out about Mickie and Felicity, he told Mickie to break it off too, but Mickie wouldn't break it off because Colin owed him. Something to do with fondue.

– And when did this come out?

– On the last day of *Bedlam*. All of it. It all came out. The whole film was in disarray, Donny Chapel was drunk, the actors were AWOL, and Leslie was deep into a mince addiction that had hounded him since his military service.

Harauld decided he would confront Mickie. Mickie had set up a giant Winnebago for himself on the set – it was huge. It had a secretarial pool as well as an actual pool. So Harauld walked straight past the secretaries, and in the back boudoir was Mickie, in flagrante with Felicity, and two supporting artists, who were doing much more than offering mere support.

There is a long pause. One that even Hughes might have been tempted to shorten.

– The rest you know from my book.
– It's quite a story. Why tell it now? Why didn't you say this in the book? You changed the story. You never mentioned Mickie and Felicity; or rather, you didn't say what they had done.
– Well, it has something to do with you. It's almost like talking to Harauld.

I look down, bashful.

– Thank you.
– More when you're silent. The illusion breaks when you speak. And also, Mickie's death releases the bond. You can't defame the dead. Not that I'm defaming him. He did betray Harauld. But Harauld insisted on keeping to the code, even though Mickie broke it himself. He made me solemnly swear to keep this to myself until Mickie and Colin had died. And this is that happy day.

She extends her hand, the knuckles steepled with arthritis. I take it.

– It is a happy day, is it not?

– I'm happy to have met you.

– It's time for you to go home.

– Thank you for your time.

– I would thank you for yours, but you have so much more of it than me.

– Don't get up.

– I wasn't going to. Will you write a book? A book about Harauld?

– I think so.

– Well, I wish you luck. Not that Harauld believed in luck.

TERMINUS

Dying is the only task you'll definitely complete.

Harauld Hughes

We look to artists to teach us how to live. They move us so much with their work that we examine their lives for clues. But often these selfsame artists have turned from their own lives and taken to the page, or the canvas, or the stave, precisely because they don't know how to live, except through art, which though it may reflect life, is no life in and of itself.

Hughes never knew his mother, so he sought a new one. He sought her in his work, he sought her in his life. At first, he thought Felicity could save him, but she couldn't. She couldn't even save herself. But then he found Lady Virginia. She couldn't replace his mother either. She did something far more valuable: she insisted he be himself. Held in her love, Hughes found, finally, his true self; he no longer needed to construct a false one, regardless of how brilliant, how *playful* that false one was.

The day after *Bedlam*'s collapse, in the garden of their Holland Park home, Harauld Hughes burnt everything he had ever written. All his published and unpublished work. He and Lady Lovilocke drank a toast. To freedom. To the end of debts.

Does writing come from a sense of incompleteness? An urge to find another plane – one where words can be shaped, per-fected, encoded? Hughes seemed to think so. He said what he needed to say, what he felt bidden to say. And when he felt equally bidden to silence, to turn inwards, to turn towards *home*, he listened. We have the films. We have the plays. We have the poetry. We cannot have Harauld. Not even Harauld could have Harauld. He was a gift. Lady Lovilocke knew that. She lived with that gift for over thirty years. She's still living with it now. I would like to thank her for sharing it with us all.

It's time to go home; any attempt to understand Harauld Hughes must remain unfinished. My Journey of Discovery isn't at an end; it can only begin again.

I see Harauld on the platform; he's waving: a welcome, a warning, a farewell.